Kent born author Carol M. Creasey wrote her first book about her autistic son in 1993 titled *My Life is Worth Living!* With four children to cope with, that book brilliantly reflects her struggles balancing a full family life and still giving her son the extra care he needed. Many years later, in her novel

The Power of Love, Carol drew from these same experiences to write about the life of a young 1960s mother coping with an autistic son.

As well as looking after her family, Carol has had a career as a manager in various china and glass merchandising establishments and also owned her own shop. Writing has always remained an important part in Carol's life, and since the original publication of *My Life is Worth Living!* she has published twelve novels, including four from the Alan Clarke crime series and her autobiography *Candidly Carol*. Carol has been the recipient of three Reader's Choice Awards, winning a coveted first place with the recently republished *My Life is Worth Living!*

SIR LEWIS HAMILTON'S
FINAL LAP WITH MERCEDES: 2024

An Unofficial Account from
Carol M. Creasey

UNITED WRITERS
Cornwall

UNITED WRITERS PUBLICATIONS LTD
Ailsa, Castle Gate, Penzance, Cornwall.
www.unitedwriters.co.uk

British Library Cataloguing in Publication Data:
A catalogue record for this book is
available from the British Library.

ISBN 9781852002183

Printed and bound in Great Britain by
United Writers Publications Ltd.,
Cornwall.

I dedicate this book to
Lewis Hamilton
and all he stands for,
and also his loyal fans worldwide.

The end of an era for Lewis Hamilton and
Mercedes. This is an account of the ups and downs
of his last season before he moved to Ferrari.

Contents

PART TWO

PART ONE

1

Introduction

On 7th January 1985, Lewis Carl Davidson Hamilton was born into a mixed-race family. His father, Anthony, and mother. Carmen, divorced when Lewis was two years old. Lewis stayed with his mother until he was ten years old, and was already showing great talent at go-cart racing. He then moved in with his father, stepmother Linda and three year old brother Nicholas.

Anthony had three jobs to support his son, who was showing a great talent in go-cart racing. Sadly, even at such a young age, Lewis was discovering how racist some people could be, and he was frequently told he was not welcome at the go-cart track by other boys' parents. He had an old go-cart, which his dad had endeavoured to do up for him, but they were both conscious of the fact that it paled into insignificance when competing against sons of much richer parents. Whilst the go-cart paled into insignificance, the driver didn't, frequently racing from the back of the grid and winning races. He had told his dad that was his way of 'Getting them back'.

Anthony was convinced that Lewis had a great future ahead of him as a Formula One driver. In 1995, at the age of ten,

Lewis approached Ron Dennis at an awards ceremony, and introduced himself by asking for his autograph. He said "Hi, I am Lewis Hamilton. I won the British Championship, and one day I want to be racing your cars." Ron Dennis was amused by Lewis's earnestness, and told him to come and see him in ten years, but by the time Lewis was thirteen years old, Ron had decided to sponsor him.

Lewis made his Formula One debut in 2007 at the age of twenty-two. He was teamed with double world champion Fernando Alonso at McLaren, and, to the surprise of many, not only did he outperform Alonso in some races, but he also stood on the podium nine times during his rookie season. Remarkably, he lost the championship by just one point.

His first championship came in 2008, when he won by one point in a dramatic final race in Brazil. He had to finish fifth to secure it, and in rounding the last corner and overtaking Timo Glock he moved up to that necessary 5th place. After winning his first title, Her Majesty Queen Elizabeth II awarded him an MBE.

In 2013 Lewis changed teams to Mercedes after Niki Lauda had convinced him it would be a good move. Between 2014 and 2020 he collected six more championships, equalling Michael Schumacher. He also became the highest scorer of pole positions to date with 104, and 103 wins. Previously, the record number of pole positions held by Schumacher had been 68. When Lewis achieved this, Michael's son Mick presented him with a special helmet to signify the milestone. In this same year, Lewis was voted Sports Personality of the year.

In 2021 Sir Lewis Hamilton set up a charitable foundation entitled Mission 44. It is a global foundation working to build a fairer future, in which every young person, no matter what their ethnicity, or whatever social injustice they may have suffered, can be given a chance to succeed. Lewis has chosen number 44, as it's always been the number of his car, even though, as a world champion, he could have changed it to number 1. He cares very passionately about helping others who, no matter how talented, may have been overlooked.

When away from the race track he enjoys many other activities. Having a healthy interest in all sport, he works hard at all times to maintain his fitness. He is very keen on fashion, and has always been very individual in his tastes. He is partnered with Tommy Hilfiger, running their own unique fashion brand, and he frequently wears these bold colours when arriving at the race track. He enjoys the opportunity to express himself in that way. He also has tattoos, and on his neck can be seen, 'God is Love'. He has piercings, and can frequently be seen wearing earrings. The fact that this sometimes divides opinion and attracts criticism does not worry him; very recently Charles Leclerc has spoken out to thank him for making it possible for drivers to embrace diversity, and not remain, as he described it, 'faceless' racing drivers.

Lewis also supports many charities, including world disaster funds, animal rights, gay rights, BLM and many more. He has frequently invited children with life limiting illnesses to be a guest of honour with him at the British Grand Prix.

Mercedes have partnered him with Mission 44, and in the case of very sick children, who are unable to leave their homes, they have arranged for a replica of his car to be parked outside the house, giving the sick child a brief moment of happiness whilst fighting life limiting disease.

Lewis has never wavered from speaking out against any injustice. It sometimes gets him unfavourable press, and opinions are divided amongst F1 fans about this. Some accuse him of being too political, but Mercedes have fully backed him by saying it is not political, it is basic human rights. He continues to set the best example he can to children who look up to him and may one day enter the sport, and he always encourages young talent. In spite of this, he is sometimes described as 'Marmite', people either love him and everything he stands for, or hate him. But one thing is for sure, he will go down in history, not just as an exceptionally talented driver, but as a truly caring human being.

2

Abu Dhabi 2021

It is impossible to write about Lewis Hamilton without mentioning the events of 12th December 2021, as this is all part of his story, and the reason he remains in Formula One at the age of 39.

When these events happened, Horner, team principal of the Red Bull team, remarked that it would be forgotten in a week or two, but, over two years later, it remains the biggest injustice that has ever occurred, and a huge talking point. So here I am reproducing the blog I wrote at the time:

"After the drama of the race in Jeddah, the whole nation of Formula One fans were expecting a thrilling climax to the season in Abu Dhabi. Formula One had more viewers than ever, with Channel 4 also being scheduled to broadcast the race live rather than highlights.

During the driver's conference, Toto Wolff, team principal of Mercedes, offered his hand to Horner as a token of sportsmanship, and the two men shook hands. Lewis and Verstappen were going into the race on equal points, with Max already claiming nine wins, and Lewis eight. If Lewis could win the last race he would win the championship by seven points.

In practice 1, Verstappen led and Lewis was third, after his fastest lap had been deleted due to track limits. In practice 2, after making some changes to his set-up, the Briton led comfortably up by four tenths of a second, to Ocon 2nd, Bottas 3rd, and Verstappen was 4th, trailing by six tenths.

In qualifying, for the first two sessions, it seemed Mercedes had the upper hand, but it all changed in Q3, where Verstappen found more time. He did a stunning lap, aided by a slipstream from Perez to put him on pole by four tenths of a second. When congratulating him afterwards, Lewis admitted that he could not have matched that time.

But on race day it was a different story, and all his fans were privileged to see a very dominant Lewis Hamilton. Although on the slower medium tyre, with Verstappen on the soft, he aced his start, and the only response from Verstappen was to run him off the track. But when he rejoined Lewis was ahead, and although Horner protested, Lewis did not have to give the place back, which was the right decision after yet another attempt to take him out.

Lewis dominated that race in style. Even when Perez also made some questionable moves to try and keep him behind, nothing was going to stop our fearless Briton from becoming an eight time world champion. Well, that was until Latifi crashed out and a safety car was deployed. There were only four laps left, so it was to be expected that the race would be finished under the safety car. But no, after various discussions with Horner over the radio, and Jonathon Wheatley also of Red Bull, who famously said, 'We only need one lap', Masi and the stewards decided to make up their own rules to manipulate the race to favour Red Bull. Verstappen was allowed to fit a new set of tyres without losing his place, and was put behind the Briton, who was on old worn tyres. Instructions were given to move the lapped cars out of the way, which was against the rules, and the result was obvious, Verstappen would win; and he did.

Horner has lauded Verstappen, saying he has driven brilliantly all year. But he has been allowed to get away with dirty driving which puts the whole FIA system into mockery, and because he hasn't been stopped, he will continue to do it until someone gets seriously injured.

Mercedes are so incensed by the breaking of the rules, they have lodged two petitions, which were thrown out by the stewards, but they may continue to fight it further. Lewis, always the gentleman, congratulated Verstappen, as did Anthony, his father, proving what class they have. Lewis also asked Mercedes not to contest the result, as he does not want to win a championship in a courtroom. Nevertheless, I can understand that knowing the Briton has faced this sort of unjust treatment all his life, they want to support him all they can.

The internet is alight with support for our Briton, who fought fairly all year long, and many are calling him the true champion, including prominent celebrities such as Nicola Adams, Piers Morgan, Gary Lineker, Serena Williams and Nick Knowles, just to name a few.

Michael Masi and the FIA should hang their heads in shame, but I doubt they will. My congratulations do go to Max Verstappen, the only driver to truly challenge Lewis this year, but he has had the fastest car for most of the year.

In my eyes, and many others, Sir Lewis won that championship in style. His car was improved by the end of the year, but he has to be commended for staying in touch before that with a car that was a true diva. Cheats never prosper, they say, and I do hope by next year the FIA will have sorted themselves out. This farce may well roll on in court, which is sad, because it should not be this way. But what makes me saddest of all is will we lose the greatest driver of all time, because if he is going to be prevented from winning his eighth championship then what will be the point of him staying? Yesterday, I fear, was a sad day for motor sport. Lewis was let down so badly.

I wrote this on 13th December 2021, and since then the FIA have taken action. Michael Masi, the race director who took orders from Jonathon Wheatley to change the rules to suit the Red Bull team, lost his job, an inquiry was set up, and the results were described as 'a human error', although the results of the championship were not changed.

After putting on a very brave face to the public, Lewis took himself out of the public eye for a few months. He has since described it as the most bizarre thing that ever happened to him. After leading the race the whole time for almost two hours, getting ever closer to the chequered flag, even the commentators were saying that he was about to make history by claiming his eighth championship. Then suddenly, in the last lap, it was all taken away from him, and the whole nation watching it was in utter disbelief.

On 15th December, just three days later, he was called to Windsor Castle and was knighted by Prince Charles for 'Services to Motor Sport'. The timing of that presentation was very soon after the most heartbreaking day of his life, and must have been balm to his emotional feelings of despair. Nobody knows for sure whether Lewis might have retired if he had won his eighth championship that day, or whether he would have tried to win even more. There was much speculation about the way he had been treated, and he remained away from the public eye until the new car was unveiled for 2022. This gave trolls the opportunity to accuse him of sulking, when actually he was struggling with his mental health, and finding it hard to come to terms with the fact that the sport he loved so much, and had given so much of himself to, had let him down so badly.

Because the rules had changed to favour high rake cars such as used in Red Bull, where Mercedes has always had low rake cars, in 2022 Lewis and his team mate Russell struggled to get good results for the team. At the end of the season Lewis had managed nine podiums and Russell eight.

Lewis, being the senior and more experienced driver, took it upon himself to help test the car with unusual set-ups, carrying weights, and he worked hard with his engineers to try and improve the car. Russell was given conventional set-ups. Lewis was concentrating on improving the car, rather than collecting points, and this became obvious when he finished in sixth place in the Drivers' Championship at the end of 2022.

One of the main issues with the car was bouncing, which caused both drivers much discomfort, so Mercedes spent most of 2022 trying to understand why this was and how to make the ride more comfortable, in the belief that once it was cured, the car would also be faster.

In 2023 the bouncing had been cured, but the car was not fast. So when Lewis actually stated that the engineers had not listened to him when he told them what was needed, this became a pivotal moment. Mercedes abandoned their zero pod design, which did not seem to be helping. James Allison was brought back to the team and a new path was taken with the development of the car.

In 2023 Lewis came third in the Drivers' Championship,

only beaten by the Red Bull drivers. Once again the car was a handful to drive, and very difficult to set up. James Allison, the designer, had returned to Mercedes to see if he could improve the car concept for 2024.

In the meantime, Lewis had signed a new contract with Mercedes to continue with them until the end of 2025 because he still wanted that eighth championship.

Verstappen, in the Red Bull car, had dominated for the last two years, his car being so fast he just drove away in every race, and in 2023, particularly, he won all but two of the races. It seemed that the Red Bull car designer, Adrian Newey, had produced the most dominant car on the grid.

When Mercedes unveiled their 2024 car, and it was tested, both Lewis and Russell said it felt much better to drive. But before that happened, in February 2024, it was announced that Lewis was going to Ferrari in 2025, to finish his Formula One career. He would then be 40 years old.

It is interesting to note that when the news of this change came out, even though it was not happening until 2025, Ferrari's share prices shot up massively overnight; such is the power of Sir Lewis Hamilton.

He had explained that it had been the hardest decision he had ever made, and there had been a clause in his contract which allowed him to do this. He also vowed to deliver during his last season with his Mercedes family, he really wanted to go out on a high.

Although fans were sad to see him leave Mercedes, finishing his career by driving for Ferrari would be the perfect ending to such an illustrious career. Toto Wolff had been very understanding about it, saying he understood that Lewis would be looking for a new challenge in the time he has left in

Formula One. Lewis and Toto have always enjoyed a very close relationship as friends, both on and off the track, so it's obvious they will miss each other. This is likewise the case between Lewis and Bono, his engineer, and it is not known yet whether Bono will be able to go with him, or whether Lewis will have a new engineer.

There are many unknowns in taking a big step like this after twelve years with the same team. However, in the meantime, 2024 would be the last year Lewis would be racing for Mercedes, and it would undoubtedly be the end of a very special era.

3

Bahrain

Lewis Hamilton's first race of 2024 was going to be in Bahrain. When the teams all unveiled their cars, Mercedes' new car for 2024 was viewed with interest by other teams. Lewis and George both reported that it felt like a proper racing car. During the second practice there was reason for optimism for the fans when Lewis topped the sheets, with George some two tenths behind him.

But it didn't quite go to plan in qualifying, as Lewis set up his car for race pace, which meant his single lap pace was not fast enough, so he qualified in 9th position. George had a different set-up and managed to qualify in 3rd position, with Verstappen on pole and Leclerc 2nd.

The race started at 3pm on Saturday, as it was Ramadan, the Islamic holy month. This would also apply next time in Jeddah. Unfortunately, the race was not a good one for the Mercedes' team owing to car problems. Their cars were overheating, so they had to lift and coast, and they also suffered with battery problems. For Lewis, as if that wasn't enough, his seat, which was now set in a much better position, became loose, and he reported that it was broken. The reply to him was 'copy', as it was not the sort of repair that could be done during a pit stop.

Later in the race, when his battery had recovered, he said he was feeling 'racy'. Unfortunately it was too late to make much headway, although he did overtake Alonso, and undercut Piastri during his pit stop, finishing in 7th position. George had hoped for a podium finish, but due to the faults with the car, slipped down to 5th place. Verstappen continued his dominant form, winning comfortably, with Perez 2nd and Sainz in 3rd.

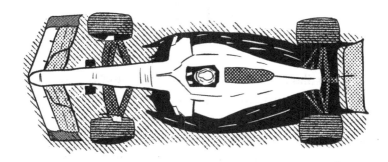

When interviewed afterwards, Lewis explained that the race was not representative of their pace, as they were literally nursing their cars and doing their utmost to get them home without a mechanical breakdown.

Many fans reacted angrily, saying that things were no different to last year, but Lewis explained it was a new car and they were just getting used to it, so no matter how disappointed fans may be, they needed to cut Mercedes some slack. They had worked incredibly hard through the winter to produce an improved car, and both the drivers indicated this was the case. It takes a few races to get the feel of a changed car, so fans were interested to see just how well they would fare at the following weekend's race in Saudi Arabia. Lewis was particularly keen to end his last season with Mercedes on a high note, so he would be giving it everything, as he always does.

4

Jeddah

Lewis Hamilton and George Russell both struggled to get a good set-up for their cars in the second race of the season in Jeddah. Toto Wolff described it as being on a knife-edge, and sometimes, for no apparent reason, the set-up fails.

Qualifying was difficult, although Russell appeared to be a little bit more comfortable in the car than Lewis, who explained that he cannot commit to the corners, and he does not have full trust in the car. Russell qualified 7th and Lewis was 8th, but they both hoped that, with a good race pace, they could climb higher up the order.

Carlos Sainz of Ferrari was diagnosed with appendicitis, and had to have an operation immediately, and 18 year old Ollie Bearman was chosen to take his place on the grid. He had qualified in 11th place on the grid.

The race started, and immediately Verstappen set off from pole position. Leclerc followed, but eventually had to concede 2nd place to Perez in the other Red Bull car. Stroll crashed his car into the barrier and luckily was unhurt. This triggered a safety car, and although Lewis was temporarily 3rd afterwards, it actually ruined any chance of him making any headway because he had to pit later.

Piastri wanted to pass him, and as Piastri was on fresh tyres, and Lewis was on worn ones, it seemed likely he would succeed. But the determination of Lewis to hold him off resulted in a masterclass of defending, and eventually Piastri had to admit defeat.

At the end of the race, Russell was in 6th place, and Lewis 9th, which made for a very disappointing result for them both. Verstappen and Perez were 1st and 2nd, and Charles Leclerc made up the final place on the podium.

But undoubtedly the star of the day was young Ollie Bearman, who climbed up from 11th to 7th place in the Ferrari. Lewis showed his admiration of the young talented driver by driving round beside him in the cool down lap, giving him a thumbs up sign, and he was the first person to greet Ollie as he got out of his car, and give him a hug of congratulation. Ollie said afterwards that he had helped him from the car, as he had trouble getting out of it after the gruelling race.

When interviewed by the press afterwards, Lewis explained that Mercedes have still got a lot of work to do to make the car more competitive. After working closely with the team to help to improve it, and knowing this was the 3rd year of difficulties, it was a sad moment to see his eyes full of anxiety. But this man never gives up, and he once again thanked everyone at the factory, saying the team will continue to keep working to make the improvements necessary.

5

Australia

When the drivers arrive at the racetrack, they usually attend a press conference, and inevitably a lot of the questions are directed at Lewis Hamilton. He is rarely non-committal in his answers, and he has no fear in standing up for what he believes in.

It had recently been announced that the FIA were carrying out an investigation about Susie Wolff, wife of Toto, who supported the inclusion of women in motor sport. As she was the managing director of the all female F1 Academy, the FIA believed there was a conflict of interest, and that she was passing information to her husband. They stated that the other teams had complained about this.

As soon as this was announced, all the teams denied they had complained at all and reiterated their trust in Susie and Toto Wolff. Susie was concerned that the publicity would ruin her good name and reputation that she had worked so hard to set up, so she decided to take them to a French court.

At the press conference, Lewis accused the FIA of having 'A lack of accountability'. He also praised Susie for having the courage to file a complaint. He stated: 'There is no transparency, there is clearly no accountability, and we need that. I think the fans need that. How can you trust the sport if we don't have that?'

Everyone is now waiting for Susie to have her day in court, and hopefully an apology for being falsely accused.

A spokesman for Mercedes had stated, after the first two races, that the car had fundamental issues, and they would be working hard for the next two weeks to try and resolve the problem. The team collected data, and studied it very carefully, to try and understand as much as possible about the car in an effort to make it go faster.

Then, during the week, it was announced they would be testing set-ups in Australia. It was becoming clearer, after three years of difficulties, that the new regulations did not suit the Mercedes, which was a low rake car.

Lewis said the car felt all right in practice 1, but not particularly fast, and he was 9th on the time sheets, whereas George was 3rd. But in practice 2, Mercedes opted to give him a test set-up, and his car was altered to such a degree that it was unsafe. It didn't hold the corners properly, and after setting a time right down in 18th place, Lewis confessed that the car had been the worst he had ever known, and he really didn't feel safe driving it.

Mercedes put out a statement afterwards explaining that they had made a massive mistake in his extreme set-up, and all the fans could hope was that it would be rectified for 3rd practice, and qualifying on Saturday. It was certainly surprising that a team that had won eight Constructors' Championships and seven Drivers' Championships could now be struggling so much.

b

In the meantime, Carlos Sainz of Ferrari, after having his appendix out only two weeks earlier, was back in his car for practice. He confessed to being worn out afterwards, so nobody knew whether he would be fit enough to drive on Sunday. Ultimately it would be his doctor who made the final decision about that.

In the third and final practice, Lewis felt more comfortable with the car, which made him feel more hopeful about qualifying. But during qualifying, after making it through to Q2, he missed out getting into Q3, and ended up in 11th place. Russell made it into the top 10, ending up in 7th position. Verstappen took pole with Sainz a fine 2nd and Perez in 3rd. Afterwards Perez lost that position when he was given a three place penalty for impeding.

When being interviewed following the practice, Lewis was visibly lacking in confidence when he explained that the way the car behaves messes with his mind. Sometimes a good race pace seems to be there, but at other times the set-up and balance just doesn't work. In contrast, Russell says he feels comfortable in the car, but it just lacks performance.

The reactions of the fans at seeing Lewis so down was anger that he was being put through such uncertainty for the third year running, but there were others who advised caution. The work at the factory had been non-stop in trying to improve this car. It just seemed hard to find that sweet spot to enable them to achieve the results that they wanted.

Toto Wolff had expressed his frustration at these results, but not with his drivers. He had frequently stated that they had the best two drivers on the grid in Mercedes, but nobody can win races, or achieve podiums, with a car that is difficult to drive. On Sunday, in the race, no doubt Mercedes would be collecting more data in an effort to improve their car for the rest of the season.

Sunday was a beautiful day. The sun was shining, and Lewis, when interviewed as the drivers' parade took place, was in optimistic mode. When the race started, Lewis overtook Alonso for 10th place. Meanwhile Verstappen led off with Carlos Sainz in hot pursuit. It wasn't long before the Spaniard had overtaken him, and the crowd cheered. But soon it became apparent that Verstappen had a problem with his car. Smoke was billowing out of it, and he headed for the pits, and on reaching them his car was on fire. It turned out to be a problem with his handbrake, but it ended his hopes of finishing the race.

Lewis was on soft tyres, so he had to pit quite early for a tyre change, and he came out in 13th place. He started to make his way up the grid until he was 10th, but then disaster struck on lap 17 when he had a sudden engine failure due to his PU unit. This came without any warning, so he had to pull off in a safe place and retire the car.

George Russell, on the penultimate lap, crashed his car into the barrier, sustaining a great deal of damage. Luckily he was OK. Later, Alonso, who was running in front of him, was given a twenty second penalty and three penalty points on his licence for 'dangerous driving'. Opinions were divided about whether this was fair, with Alonso himself saying he had brake problems, and some people felt George had badly misjudged the corner in a car that was not stable round bends.

Carlos Sainz, who, as already mentioned, had just recovered from an appendix operation, drove a fine race and fully deserved the win. Leclerc was 2nd and Norris of McLaren was 3rd. Carlos was also voted the driver of the day.

Toto Wolff was in despair for his drivers and his team. Lewis, when interviewed, was calm, and he commented that it was the worst start to the year he had ever had. With two retirements Mercedes had hit rock bottom, but the only way to go after that was up, and they vowed to dust themselves up and get back to scoring points again. 'Still I rise' means exactly that.

6

Ferrari Beckons

The whole of Formula One reacted with amazement when it was announced that Lewis Hamilton would be driving for Ferrari in 2025. In fact, many people were in disbelief. Rumours abound all the time in the world of motor racing. The press often embroider stories about drivers both in and out of the car, just to get clicks on their articles.

Of course, one of the first people that Lewis told was his boss and friend Toto Wolff. Lewis went for his Christmas break, but unbeknown to the world of motor sport, John Elkhan, the president of Ferrari, and Fred Vasseur, who had previously coached Lewis when he was in McLaren, were both in contact with him, and making their intentions very clear.

Although the second oldest driver on the grid after Alonso at 42, Lewis had lost none of his motivation and enthusiasm. In 2023, with a difficult car, he still managed to beat every other driver on the grid except the Red Bull drivers, claiming 3rd place in the Drivers' Championship.

But the ghost of 2021 remained. That eighth championship that many felt was taken away from him; and it still remains no secret that he wants to achieve this before he retires. Since 2023

Ferrari had been getting faster, and appeared to be closer to Red Bull than any other team. Indeed, with Verstappen's retirement from the race in Australia, Ferrari managed to capitalise on this and claim 1st and 2nd place.

Lewis and Toto wanted him to win his eighth championship with Mercedes, it would have been a fitting end to a great partnership, and Toto reminded the fans that 'We owe him a championship.'

Of course, it was too early to know whether Mercedes could solve the problems with their new car, and find the performance that they needed. Lewis has described this as his worst start to the season since 2009, but these sort of obstacles did not faze him or Mercedes. They had spent the last three years trying to understand their very complex car, after previously winning for seven years in a row.

Toto admitted that he was as surprised as anyone that Lewis was going to Ferrari, although Lewis made sure to tell him immediately he had signed the contract. Usually drivers make a decision to change teams at the end of the season, they do not announce it a year beforehand, but Lewis explained that he could not have carried the emotional burden of knowing he was leaving without sharing it.

Right from the beginning, Toto said he understood, and both Mercedes' drivers would be treated equally during Lewis's final year. He joked with Lewis saying that he doesn't think red suits him. They have that sort of relationship. But although Mercedes had not started the year very well, there was plenty of time to improve, and the engineers at the factory continued with their efforts to refine the car.

Formula One can be a cut-throat environment, and it's believed that a driver is only as good as their last race. The press had already named several drivers who they believed might take Lewis's place next year. Toto had capitalised on the power struggle going on at Red Bull between Horner and Marko by jokingly offering both Marko and Verstappen a place in his team.

All this banter continues throughout the year. Its normal for the press to speculate about who will be where, but nobody would know for sure until the end of the season, and when this book is finished, all will be revealed. The only thing known for sure is that Lewis is going to Ferrari in 2025.

7

Japan

The world of Formula One is no different to anywhere else when it comes to gossip and rumours. The press seize on everything and produce their own version of events, or speculate, which is sometimes misleading, and very occasionally correct.

Ever since Lewis announced he would be going to Ferrari in 2025, speculation had been rife about who would take his seat at Mercedes. Sainz had certainly proved his worth as a fast driver, and would be without a team next year. Toto Wolff had noted a young man of 17 named Andrea Kimi Antonelli, who was showing great promise, but Toto had publicly stated that he might be too young to join in 2025. The pressure at such a young age may be something he was not yet ready for.

Then there was Alonso, who continued to prove that age is no barrier. In 2025 he will be 43 years old, but he remains a very fast driver. Would it be fitting for him to join Mercedes? As well as speed, team leaders try to put drivers together who will gel and support each other. So, as Toto expected to make Russell the team leader, it would be hard to imagine Alonso wanting to be second to someone who was his junior by more than fifteen years.

All these questions and scenarios are inevitably asked of the drivers and the team principals during the press day, which takes place on Thursday, and whatever answer the press get will form the basis of the articles they will write about the race weekend.

Another important question is what a driver might feel about how his car will perform, as circuits vary considerably. When Lewis was asked this question in Japan, he said he didn't know for sure what to expect, as they have not yet discovered the sweet spot when setting the car up, but they are continuing to work on it. Another curve ball to be thrown into the equation was the weather forecast. Rain was expected on Sunday during the race, so anything could happen.

There had been a rumour that Sebastian Vettel, who retired in 2022, was thinking about coming back. Vettel himself confirmed that he had been approached, and at the moment was weighing up his options. Lewis was delighted to hear this news, as they had been friends for years, and Vettel had supported him in his stand for inclusion in motor sport. They spent the years from 2017-2019 battling each other on the track when Vettel was in Ferrari, being very evenly matched at times, but Lewis beat him each time to the championship, and Sebastian was the first person to say that Lewis fully deserved to win.

Lewis liked the idea of Sebastian coming to Mercedes to take his place, and he pointed out to the press what a worthy candidate he would be because his values and example would align with those of Mercedes, and help to create a happy working relationship with George Russell.

During first practice, track conditions were normal. George and Lewis set times 4th and 5th fastest respectively, and this did much to boost their confidence. But in practice 2 it was raining hard and a mere handful of cars went out. Lewis wanted to test the track in these conditions, so he did a lap on soft tyres, which put him 2nd to Piastri from McLaren. Russell and Verstappen did not go out at all.

Afterwards, when interviewed, Lewis was very happy, and he said the car was the best that its had been for three years. He also thanked his mechanics profusely for all the hard work that had gone into making the car more drivable. He said the car appeared to be set up right, so was hoping there would be no more changes before qualifying.

Qualifying was better for Lewis this time. Indeed, at the end of Q2 he was 3rd on the time sheets. Obviously, at times like this, the fans feel uplifted, but in Q3 the times were so close to each other, that Lewis ended up 7th and George 9th. It was pointed out afterwards by Toto, that if Lewis had been just a tenth of a second quicker, he would have been lining up on the second row, instead of the 4th. Although the Red Bull car was far ahead, the teams of Mercedes, McLaren and Ferrari were very close to one another in performance, with some tracks suiting certain cars more than others.

On race day, the fans, having seen Lewis with a much more confident demeanour in practice and qualifying, were full of hope that he could make progress up the grid from 7th.

The weather was kind, a sunny day, and when the race started all eyes were peeled. There was a crash between Ricciardo and Albon, which also damaged the barriers, and the race was red flagged. Luckily both drivers were unhurt. It was some time before racing could be resumed, and in the meantime, Lewis took advantage of the free pit stop to put on hard tyres.

Lewis Fan Photographs

From top left: Emma Junus, Benjamin Dowling, Josephine Jackson, Debbie White, Kais Hameed, Larry Sarpong.

Unfortunately this did not work for him, as he then had oversteer, and the tyres degraded really quickly.

Time-wise, for Lewis and George, the first stint was very slow, as they both suffered the same problem. Lewis was suffering more, and he volunteered to let George through so that the team would get more points. If he had not, it was unlikely that George would have been able to pass him safely, and then maybe neither of them would have been in the top ten to collect points. This display of being a team player, rather than for oneself, was surely a good example to some of the up and coming future champions, who sometimes forget, when they are battling fiercely, that they are racing for their team, and not just themselves.

Naturally there was huge disappointment from the fans that Lewis was now languishing down in 9th place, and George in a lowly 7th, which was the reverse of where they qualified, but the nature of the track at Suzuka was never going to favour Mercedes.

When interviewed afterwards, Lewis was trying hard to hide his disappointment, because earlier in the weekend he had felt optimistic of his chances to achieve a podium finish. But his body language spoke for him, especially when a reporter asked him a question which was not at all relevant this year, when he was doing his best to help team Mercedes. The question was. 'Are you jealous of Ferrari, now they are doing so well.' Carlos Sainz had come 2nd in the race, and Charles Leclerc 4th. Lewis was not impressed. He is a man who normally tolerates most questions, but that reporter had got under his skin.

'Have you not got any better questions to ask,' he retorted, and with that he left the room.

Fans had to keep faith in Mercedes, they had a car with a

completely new concept, and Lewis felt he was just getting to grips with it. They would be developing it during the year, and progress would be made. Lewis wanted to end his time with Mercedes on a high, so the loyalty of his fans to him, and to his team who helped him win so many championships in the past, was needed now more than ever.

Many fans were disgruntled at what they felt was a lack of progress, but it was easy to sit in an armchair and criticise. The engineers at the factory were working long hours, and they deserved respect for all the hard work that went on. In the meantime, here they were with hope in their hearts that they could improve the car.

8

China

The last time China hosted a Formula One race was 2019. It was scheduled for 2020, but then Covid 19 arrived and it had to be cancelled. In 2019, Bottas, the former team mate of Lewis at Mercedes, took pole position with Lewis 2nd. Vettel of Ferrari was 3rd, Leclerc 4th and Verstappen 5th.

Lewis won the race, some 6 seconds ahead of Bottas, who was 2nd. Vettel made up the final position on the podium of 3rd, with Verstappen in 4th place and Leclerc in 5th.

This was during the days when Mercedes was a competitive car, which lasted until 2021. In recent years, the brilliance of Adrian Newey, the designer at Red Bull, has become very evident, as he has created a car which is so fast that it is in its own race. Verstappen just drives away, and nobody else can keep up with him.

However, the one flaw with all this, which doesn't go down well with fans of Formula One, who expect fair play, was that in 2022 Red Bull breached the regulations and overspent on the budget cap, which had been introduced to make racing fairer. Their punishment was a reprimand from Ben Sulayem, F1 president, and a sporting fine, which involved a reduction in wind tunnel time, which was described by Horner at the time as a 'Draconian punishment'.

However, throughout 2024 Formula One, it was the Red Bull era, which means all teams were having to work even harder to catch up and pass them. But, out of the top teams, Mercedes was the one that was struggling the most with the new regulations. They worked hard to try and eradicate all their problems and become more competitive.

During the week before the Chinese Grand Prix, there were two items of news for the fans. Fernando Alonso of the Aston Martin team, whose contract was due to finish at the end of the season in December, signed a two year contract with them until 2026. There had been much speculation about him, as he mentioned retirement, but now his future is sealed until the end of 2026. He will be 45 years old by then, but last year he was one place behind Lewis in the Drivers' Championship, in 4th place, which meant, apart from the two Red Bull drivers, Lewis and Alonso, the more senior drivers, had beaten all the younger men, some of them as much as twenty years younger.

The other item of news was concerning the life of Lewis away from Formula One. He attended the GQ Global Creativity Awards, which were held in New York City. It was decided to honour Sir Lewis at this very prestigious event, and he was given the title of Transcending Powerhouse, which is in recognition of his support of people of colour, females in sport, and LQBTQIA . He has made it very clear that he wants to help work on diversity within the sport, so, to enable that, he has started his project, which is Mission 44. This was originally set up in 2021, and it continues to go from strength to strength.

The weather forecast for China was one showing changing conditions for the weekend, which can sometimes spice things up. However, there were murmurs of discontent from Perez, Verstappen and Norris that they were returning to a race track that they had not raced at for five years, which would have a new surface, and it had been decided to hold the first sprint race of the year. They felt that only one practice session would be a disadvantage, but, in actual fact, all the drivers would be in the same boat.

In the first practice Mercedes decided to do something different and they got both Lewis and George to run on hard tyres whilst other teams were vying for fast laps. The fact that they finished 17th and 18th on the time sheet didn't mean much, as they had literally just been testing the tyres, and not chasing speed.

Later came the sprint qualifying, and conditions were dry. Both Lewis and George made it into Q2, Lewis was 9th and George 11th. Unfortunately George could not improve, so he did not make it out of Q2. Lewis just made it into Q3. Suddenly it started raining, and cars were aquaplaning all over the track. Several went off, including Leclerc and Norris, who had his lap time deleted, which was the fastest. Lewis, who has always loved the challenge of driving in the rain, put in a stunning lap, which gave him pole position, briefly. McLaren appealed against Norris's lap being deleted, so it was reinstated with Lewis now 2nd. Both of the Britons had done incredible drives in such dangerous conditions. Alonso was 3rd, and Verstappen 4th.

Lewis was in buoyant mood when being interviewed

afterwards, explaining how his car seemed to thrive in the cooler conditions. But he also added a caution that if Saturday was dry, then the faster Red Bulls and Ferraris were likely to overtake him. But if it rained again, it was down to the skill of the driver rather than the car, so he might get a good result. I am sure all his fans prayed for rain.

Saturday was a fine and dry day. When the race started, Lewis challenged Norris for the lead, and was soon past him. He led the race until the 9th lap, but by then, Verstappen had caught up and passed him. Lewis hung on grimly to 2nd place, even Perez in the other Red Bull could not catch him. Verstappen was some 13 seconds ahead by the 19th lap, and Perez was just 2 seconds behind. Contrary to the expectations of Lewis, the Ferraris and the McLarens were unable to match his pace. Perez made up the 3rd place on the podium, so Lewis had come 2nd.

This was a far better result than he had expected with the car, and, of course, his fans were jubilant, many taking to social media to express their delight at his 2nd place result.

But sadly his euphoria was short lived, as he had set up his car differently for the qualifying round of the main race, taking it in a completely different direction with a view to understanding it better. It did not work, as he lost grip and locked up, then finding himself down in 18th place, he was unable to get out of Q1.

When interviewed after, he kept his good humour and laughed off his disappointment, stating that he was going to have fun on Sunday racing from the back of the grid. He said if it was rainy, it would be good, but no rain was forecast for Sunday.

Sunday was dry, and when the race started, although Lewis

was on soft tyres, he could not seem to get them to work for him, and he lost a place at the start. After a while it was a bit better, and he made up places, but then went in for an early pit stop. There was a safety car and a virtual safety car, Bottas had to retire with an engine problem, and the virtual safety car gave Lewis the opportunity to pit again, and not lose as much time as a normal pit stop would. After the stop he came out again in 19th place, and had it all to do again.

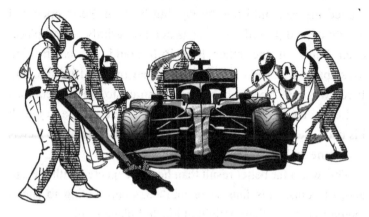

He gradually climbed up the order with some fine overtakes, making it to 8th position. But Alonso had pitted for fresh tyres, and he overtook Lewis, who then had to settle for 9th position. It had been a sterling effort by the Briton, who seemed to have better pace at the end of the race. Of course, we will never know if he could have made it to the podium if he had qualified higher.

Verstappen won by some thirteen seconds, even after two safety cars had closed up the grid. Norris was a fine 2nd, and Perez was 3rd. The Ferrari duo were 4th and 5th, but mystified as to why their pace seemed to be lacking at this circuit. Russell was 6th and Alonso 7th.

At this point the fans became desperate to see Lewis doing well in his final year with Mercedes. They believed that Mercedes had changed towards Lewis because he was leaving the team. But Toto promised to treat both his drivers equally, and he is a man of integrity. Nevertheless, sadly, after three years of hoping the car will be competitive, the fans had lost some faith in Mercedes, suggesting they didn't trust them any more.

But Lewis still believed the team could turn it around, and it was a long season. An upgrade was coming to Miami, and Lewis had said he will never run that weird qualifying set-up again, because it didn't work. All eyes would be on Mercedes once again to see if they could deliver for their drivers. Such pressure must be a bit overwhelming. But for Lewis, who had won in China more times than any driver, having been successful six times, it must have been very frustrating. His determination remained unchanged, he still believed in Mercedes, so any improvements or developments that could be utilised in Miami would be gratefully received by Lewis and George.

At least Lewis could take away from his weekend in China, not only a runner up position in the sprint race, but also the memory of the overwhelming love and support afforded to him by the Chinese fans. Maybe this support helped him when he was racing from the back of the grid to make it into the top ten.

9

Miami

Any large organisation that has many people working within it has its share of rumours and stories, which are passed around very quickly, and the world of Formula One is no exception. The press are always looking for stories, and there is a very thin line between a rumour and a true story. The pundits and the press are very harsh on drivers if they perform below expectations, and one often wonders why these armchair critics, who know nothing about Formula One, feel the need to be like this, but, of course, they feel it makes a good story.

Less than a week after the Chinese Grand Prix, rumours started circulating that Adrian Newey, designer for Red Bull, wanted to leave the team. This had been written before, and many people reading it marked it as 'clickbait', which is a way that journalists get people to read their articles which are mainly unsubstantiated.

But for three days these headlines dominated social media, and were then reported by BBC Sports News and Sky News, who are both regarded as reliable sources. The reason for him wanting to leave was said to be that he likes a calm environment to work in, and the continuing power struggle between Horner and Marko, and the fact that the Austrian part of the company and the Thai side are divided, had made him want to quit. The final straw appeared to be the controversy that Horner found himself in, and as Horner had refused to step down from his position, the drama continued to drag on and take the focus off racing.

Adrian Newey himself made no comment, but reliable sources had stated that his contract ran until 2025, but if he could buy himself out, he would like to leave at the end of the 2024 season. It seems his relationship with Horner and the team had soured over time.

There were more speculations about where he might be heading next. He was supposedly meeting with Mercedes after the Miami Grand prix, along with Verstappen, to speak about the future. Another piece of information was that Aston Martin had already offered him an undisclosed, but huge amount, of money to join them. He had turned it down. Others believed that as he had previously stated that his one regret was not working with Lewis Hamilton, he might have been negotiating a deal to join him at Ferrari for the next year. The final option was that at 65 he may wish to retire, and concentrate his time on the boat he had designed. In the meantime, Red Bull had issued a statement saying they had not had notice from Adrian about leaving, and he was contracted to stay until the end of 2025.

It had been pointed out that, even if he could leave in 2024, he would have to take a year of gardening leave, which means he would not be available until 2026, the year when the regulations change, and he would have missed the opportunity as the car would have been designed in 2025.

Until an official announcement was made, nobody knew what the future may hold, but if he did leave Red Bull, it was believed that others would follow him. The next piece of information from supposedly reliable sources was that he had brought lawyers in to help him to negotiate a deal to leave Red Bull at the end of the 2024 season.

Meanwhile, whilst all these rumours continued to swirl, Toto Wolff, together with Lewis Hamilton, went to the Empire State Building to meet up with representatives of Whatsapp, who they are partners with, and reveal their new emoji car. Toto and Lewis pressed a button to light up the Empire State Building in green, and both made warm speeches about being there. Lewis drove his Formula One car down 5th Avenue, and then did doughnuts with it, to the delight of the fans who flocked to see him.

On Wednesday 1st May, an official announcement was made by Red Bull stating that Adrian Newey, who has been with them since 2006, would be leaving. It also stated that he was presently with his lawyers, negotiating when his exit would be. Later in the day, another announcement was given that he was going to step back from his duties immediately, and concentrate on the RB17 hypercar project. This apparently meant he was no longer part of the team, and was classed as his 'gardening leave'. He would then leave the team altogether in 2025, and be free to start another project.

Any team on the grid would want to have this engineering genius working to design a car for their team, although the teams mentioned as a possibility were Mercedes, Aston Martin and Ferrari. Aston Martin offered him a big sum of money, which he turned down, and Mercedes did not approach him, as their chief engineer James Allison had recently returned, and had his own contract in place. This left Ferrari, who had not had a championship win since the early 2000s.

Newey had stated before that he would have loved to have worked with Lewis Hamilton, but that was a few years earlier, and as he now had his own sailing yacht, maybe retirement was his favourite option. Meanwhile the world of Formula One, particularly fans of Lewis Hamilton, were waiting with bated breath to see what would happen. When asked about this possibility at the drivers' conference, Lewis said it would be an honour and a privilege to work with him, and if he had to make a list, Newey would be right at the top of it. The smile he gave afterwards might have given his fans hope that a deal had already been struck secretly.

Toto announced that in an effort to improve the balance of the car, Mercedes had added some updates. All eyes of the fans were on them during practice to see if there was any difference, and afterwards Lewis and George both reported that the car felt a bit better. However, when it came to qualifying for the sprint race, to their great disappointment, neither driver was able to get out of Q2, finishing 11th and 12th. Lewis, when interviewed afterwards, expressed disappointment, but vowed he would do his utmost to get into the points, which meant he must somehow get from 12th to 8th on a street track, a course famously very tough to overtake on.

Lewis made a great start, he saw a gap and went for it, launching himself from 12th to 9th position. In the meantime Alonso had hit his team mate Stroll, and had not expected Lewis to pass him, describing in anger, that Hamilton had arrived like a bull. After the impact from Alonso, Stroll then hit Norris, which finished his race. Norris complained afterwards that Hamilton had ruined his race, but when the stewards looked at the incident, it was clear that Alonso's move on Stroll had caused the problem, and it was deemed a racing incident. Later in the race, when Lewis was attempting to overtake Magnussen, he did some unsporting defending, having run Lewis off the track twice in an effort to protect his team mate Hulkenberg from being overtaken and losing points. Magnussen was later given a twenty second penalty for dirty driving. By the end of the race Lewis had got himself up to 8th place, earning one point, but after the race he was also given twenty seconds penalty for apparently speeding in the pit lane. Many fans questioned the harshness of the decision because, in the past, drivers were usually fined for this. It did seem to them a very biased decision.

When he was interviewed afterwards, Lewis was in good spirits, and laughed when he was told that Magnussen had admitted his own driving had been atrocious. He told the reporter that it was fine, and because he loves racing, how much he had enjoyed the race. He then shrugged his shoulders and admitted that it did suck to lose the point, but he was grinning at the same time. So his overall position after the penalty was 16th and George was 12th, so neither of them scored any points.

Qualifying for the main race later was better. Lewis did a stunning lap in Q2 to claim 2nd, but in Q3 he couldn't get his tyres to work, and ended up 8th with George in 7th, but at least this time they had made it into the top ten.

On race day, once again Lewis got a good start, which saw him up to 7th position. He had overtaken Nico Hulkenberg, who was on medium tyres, whereas Lewis was on hard. But soon after Hulkenberg took the place back from Lewis. The Briton wasn't standing for that, and overtook him again, this time managing to keep his position, and stretch out a lead. There was a virtual safety car, and then a full safety car later in the race, which enabled Norris of McLaren to get a free pit stop and take the lead.

When the race started again after the safety car, Verstappen was right behind Norris in 2nd, and the fans expected him to overtake Lando Norris and take the lead again, but it soon became clear that the pace of the McLaren was faster. By the end of the race Norris had stretched out a lead of seven seconds, which Verstappen was unable to do anything about. He accepted 2nd, and praised Norris for his first win. It was many years since McLaren had won a race, and Lando Norris had waited patiently for five years to get his first one, so it was well done to him!

Lewis looked racy, and although the car was not as fast as the others, he battled his way up to 6th, his highest position so far in 2024. When interviewed after, he praised his engineers for giving him a good set-up. It was definitely a step up from 9th, which was heartening. George Russell was not happy with his day, he slipped to 8th place and finished seventeen seconds behind Lewis.

But the good news for Formula One fans was that Red Bull could be beaten, although Horner had stated that Max damaged the floor of his car when he hit the cone, and so lost performance. It was now sure all eyes would be on Red Bull and McLaren in two weeks time at Imola.

c

10

Imola

One week after Miami, and people were still talking about Newey's sudden exit from Red Bull, and also speculating about what he would do next. Would he take on another project, and join a rival team, or would he retire?

During that same week, news emerged that two of Mercedes staff were leaving to join Lewis Hamilton at Ferrari. Jerome D'Ambrosio, who was currently deputy team principal, and took up the reins when Toto Wolff was temporarily laid up when he had a knee operation. Loic Serrais, the other one, was Head of Chassis Performance Engineering. They would both debut in the new team in October. They had been brought over by Fred Vasseur, who was doing everything he could to strengthen his team and provide Lewis with familiar faces to work with.

Mercedes brought the second part of their upgrades with them, and Lewis admitted that he was excited about seeing if they improved the performance of the car. During the week, he also said that he still had so much love for the team. After twelve years with them, it was hardly surprising. Whether there would be enough of an improvement in the competitiveness of the car so that he could scoop some wins before he moved to Ferrari was unknown at the moment, only time would tell.

Sebastian Vettel was present at the track that weekend, and he organised a tribute run around Imola in memory of Ayrton Senna, who was tragically killed whilst competing there thirty years earlier, and also Roland Raztenberger. This is what he said: 'The idea is to do a lap with all the other drivers and the paddock to remember Ayrton and Roland. Then we will stop at Tamburello. We have these little padlocks made to lock our thoughts; to take a moment to remember what inspired us, what we associate with the name of Ayrton Senna, and to lock the padlock here on the barriers.'

Vettel also gave the drivers bright yellow tee shirts to wear with 'Forever' inscribed on them. Lewis has always named Ayrton Senna as his inspiration, and his death, at the age of 34, remains forever a tragedy which robbed the Formula One world of a gifted driver, who was still competing at the highest level on that fateful day. Nobody knows whether he could have won more than the three championships he had already, had this not happened.

Although the weather was fine when everyone arrived, the forecast suggested there may be rain during the race on Sunday, although it was expected that it would be dry on Saturday when qualifying would take place.

Practice 1 showed some solid improvements, and finished with Russell 2nd on the time sheets, and Lewis 7th. In practice 2, Lewis was 4th and Russell 5th. Lewis was three tenths away from Leclerc who topped both sessions. But the surprise of the day was Verstappen, who seemed to struggle through both sessions, and was visibly frustrated. In 2nd practice he was 7th, although it was to be expected that Red Bull would probably solve the problem, and his car would be set up differently for the qualifying rounds.

By the time qualifying arrived, the Red Bull car had been set up differently, so Verstappen claimed pole, but this time only by a tiny margin. During his last run, he was given a slipstream by Hulkenberg, which enabled him to beat Piastri of McLaren, who was 2nd. Sadly for Piastri, he received a three place penalty for impeding, which relegated him down to 5th place. Norris, who had been 3rd, then inherited his 2nd place, with Leclerc in 3rd.

Lewis and George got through to Q3, and qualified in 8th and 6th place respectively. Once again, their car just didn't have the pace over one lap, so they both realised they had a great deal of work to do on Sunday to get further up the grid.

Sunday was a sunny and bright day, contrary to the rain that had been predicted. During the drivers' parade, Lewis spoke about how hard it was to pass on this track, and he was going to do his best to get past Tsunoda, the driver in 7th place, at the start.

Lewis performed a lightning start, and was past Tsunoda immediately, putting him just behind his team mate. Verstappen pulled away at the start, and then built up a lead of seven seconds. Unusually, there were no crashes or safety cars in this race, and because it was virtually impossible to overtake, fans who were watching described it as a 'bore fest'. But towards the end of the race, it became clear that after only one stop, Verstappen had worn his tyres out, whereas Norris, who was in 2nd position, had not. Gradually, during the last 20 laps, Norris started to reel him in, and suddenly the race became alive.

After his pit stop, Lewis came out in 9th position, he got past Stroll and Perez to get himself up to 7th, and Russell was in 6th. Lewis had also looked after his tyres, and was ready to pass Russell, who had completely worn his down. The team felt Russell was in danger of not finishing the race.

The first time they asked Russell if he wanted to pit he refused, but later they told him he must box, so he came in, and with his fresh tyres was able to get the fastest lap. This gave him an extra point. Meanwhile Lewis had then moved up to 6th, which was where he finished.

By the last lap, Norris had got his gap of seven seconds to Verstappen down to less than one second, everyone was watching with bated breath, but this time, on a track so narrow it's really hard to pass, Verstappen just managed to hold him off to claim the victory.

But what was now exciting for Formula One, was that another team had actually managed to catch up with the dominant Red Bull at last. Also Ferrari was not far behind, as Charles Leclerc took 3rd place, much to the delight of the passionate Tifosi. It was the first time a podium has happened for Ferrari at Imola since 2006. On that day it was claimed by Schumacher. Fred Vasseur said they also had upgrades, which would take time to work, but when they did, he believed that Ferrari would also be fighting Red Bull.

Mercedes would have loved to join the party, but the positive taken from this weekend was that they had made a small step forward. Lewis thanked them afterwards for all their efforts. They would continue to work steadily to improve performance and speed. In the meantime, races looked to be more closely fought, so fans could look forward to seeing proper racing. It seemed that Red Bull was no longer dominant.

For Lewis, knowing that he would be at Ferrari next year was very exciting for him. At the beginning of 2024, aware that it was his last season with Mercedes, his dearest wish was to earn his 8th title with the team that he has shared such a wonderful relationship with for the last twelve years. But unless huge strides could be made during the year, it now seemed less likely, so the next best thing he could hope for was to pick up a win or a podium as the season progressed.

However, none of these setbacks would dim Lewis's resolve to help the team, that had assisted in his achieving seven titles, get back to winning ways. He had been accused by some of 'already checking out' ahead of his move in 2025, but nothing could be further from the truth. He stayed late in the night to help the engineers with all his feedback. He spent time testing unusual set-ups in an effort to understand the car, and his race positions and qualifying had suffered because of it. He didn't care about that, or when people said he was now 'past it'. His determination and passion to win remained exactly the same. In 2024 he would remain focused on Mercedes until the very last race, and then, in 2025, when he joins with Ferrari, all his energy will be spent helping them to win because this is the sort of person he is.

11

Monaco

Monaco was the next race on the calendar, this time it was just one week later. It is an iconic racetrack, which winds through the streets of the principality, and it's also narrow. It is very hard to pass, so getting pole position is essential to have any hope of winning. Because right now their car was on a knife-edge, this would make it very hard for Mercedes to get anywhere near the front.

Many people said they wondered how the Tifosi, who are the Italian fans, would react to Lewis Hamilton being in the Ferrari team in 2025. Back in the years between 2017-2019, when Lewis was battling against Vettel of Ferrari, he beat him, and was booed by the fans, although many of them admitted then they wished he was with Ferrari.

So, in Imola, Lewis came face to face with the Tifosi, and even though he has not won a race since 2021, they greeted him rapturously. Anyone who follows Formula One knows no matter how good a driver is, if he doesn't have a competitive car, it's impossible to win races. It was heartbreaking to watch Mercedes struggle with the new regulations after eight years of winning the Constructors' Championship. Lewis had spent the last three years trying to help them get back on top. He had endured criticism and sneers because he was not winning, such was his loyalty to the team.

His decision to go to Ferrari, who courted him for a long time, was not taken lightly. His relationship with his team boss Toto Wolff was not just a business one, they were also close friends. But the desire to get his eighth title still burned brightly inside him, especially because it was taken from him on the last lap at Abu Dhabi in 2021, and he probably saw Ferrari as his last chance to fight for it.

Formula One can be a cruel sport, and many people have opinions which they are happy to vent. He has been accused of deserting a sinking ship, but after three years of trying to help, knowing that he will be 40 in 2025, he may feel his time to succeed is running out. He is at the peak of fitness, has lost none of his skills, and Ferrari have every faith in him. Fred Vasseur, team principal of Ferrari, described the impending arrival of Lewis as 'A breath of Spring'. He worked with Lewis when he was competing in the GP2 Series, Young Driver Programme. Lewis won the 2003 British Formula Renault Championship, then in 2005 Formula 3 Euro Series, and in 2006 GP2 Series, which was when Fred worked with Lewis and realised his full potential.

Fred described Lewis as a motivator, with endless energy. After the years Lewis has been in Mercedes, it is a fact that, due to having him, their profile has been raised. Fred knows this will also happen in Ferrari, as Sir Lewis Hamilton has become a global icon, not just because of his racing ability, but also because of his unwavering support of many causes, both humanitarian and also animal rights, with inclusion and diversity featuring heavily.

Some people feel he should not have these other causes in his life, they accuse him of being political, but Mercedes have always championed him by saying: 'It's not political, it's just basic human rights.'

It doesn't affect his racing life, and he states quite candidly, that whilst he is in Formula One, it gives him a platform to spread awareness of things that need to be addressed. This is what makes him different from the other drivers, and it means some fans hate him and what he stands for, whilst others love him for it. But in 2025, Fred, John Elkan and Ferrari are ready to embrace him and all he stands for.

First practice on Friday looked really promising, with Lewis top of the time sheets, followed by Russell. Then, later in the day, 2nd practice took place, and Lewis was 2nd. This form was carried through to practice 3, where he finished 3rd. He declared later that the car was great to drive, and very enjoyable. His fans were all posting on social media that he must carry this form right through to qualifying, and urging his team not to make any changes to the car and spoil the momentum.

Both Mercedes drivers got comfortably through to Q3 for the top ten shoot out, but then it became tricky because the times were all so close. Lewis was 3rd at one point, but by the end of the session he had slipped to 7th place. Russell, who was running a new front wing upgrade, which gave him two tenths of a second advantage, made it into 5th place.

When interviewed afterwards, Lewis was visibly disappointed to be down in 7th after having done so well all weekend until then. It seemed his qualifying for the rest of the year would be compromised because priority would be given to

Russell with upgrades. This was because he was leaving, and Russell was remaining there for next year.

It is usually the pole sitter who will win Monaco, as it's virtually impossible to overtake. Charles Leclerc of Ferrari took pole position, a special moment for him at his own home race, and many of the fans were delighted for him, and wished him well for Sunday. Piastri of McLaren was 2nd, and Sainz was 3rd.

Verstappen and Perez had a troubled weekend with their car set-up, as the bumps and kerbs compromised their race pace. Perez went out in Q1, and Verstappen ended up in 6th place after hitting the wall, and not going out again to try and improve his lap in Q3. It was believed that their poor performance was track specific, and would not affect them at future races.

Sunday arrived, and it was a fine day. The cars lined up, and all got away safely until the 2nd lap, then there was a massive pile-up between Perez, Hulkenberg and Magnusson, who were luckily unhurt, but forced to retire from the race. It brought out a red flag, as there was a significant amount of debris spread all around the track.

The race resumed after forty minutes. Some of the drivers took advantage of the safety car to change their tyres. Lewis had not been happy with being on the hard tyres, so he took the opportunity to change to medium tyres. Mercedes instructed Russell to stay out of the dirty air of Norris, and encouraged him to look after his tyres. This resulted in him driving slowly, which held up Verstappen, who could not pass him, and it also meant that Lewis could not attempt a pass on Verstappen.

Lewis pitted on lap 52, and was given hard tyres. Unfortunately his team did not tell him it was a critical lap to undercut Verstappen, so when it was time for Verstappen to pit, he stayed ahead of Lewis. Lewis was visibly frustrated with the team, but he did put in the fastest lap of the race, which gave him an extra point. So with no opportunities presented for anyone to overtake, which made it a bit of a procession, Lewis closed up on Verstappen, and was running less than half a second behind him, but could do nothing about it.

Charles Leclerc was a fine 1st place, Piastri 2nd, and Sainz 3rd. Russell held Verstappen off for 5th, and Lewis remained in 7th, which disappointed him a lot. When interviewed afterwards, he stated how he wished there had been opportunities to overtake. The next race was in Canada, and he vowed to give it his all when he got there.

12

Some Background History

When Lewis Hamilton won his first World Championship in 2008, he was at the time, the youngest driver to do so, being 23 years old at the time. This record was subsequently broken when Vettel won his World Championship at 22 years old with Red Bull.

Naturally all drivers want to win as many championships as they can, but Lewis's hopes of a 2nd one were dimmed when Button of Brawn GP won in 2009. Then followed the Red Bull era, where Vettel won four championships. But although McLaren had failed to produce a competitive car, Lewis became the only driver to get at least one win in every year, up until that record was broken in 2022.

After four years of McLaren producing a non competitive car, the late Niki Lauder convinced Lewis to join Mercedes in 2013, which was at that time a mid field team. Many people shook their heads in disbelief at such a move, but during the following years the Briton set out to prove everyone wrong. He won his next two championships in 2014 and 2015, and was beaten by Rosberg in 2016 by just five points. It had been a stressful year for Lewis, as his car had many reliability problems and engine failures. Luckily, by the time 2017 came, Mercedes had fixed the reliability problems on his car, and from 2017 up until and including 2020, he brought his championship tally up to seven championships, which equalled Schumacher.

Mercedes and Lewis Hamilton became a great partnership. Toto Wolff embraced his unique character, and allowed him to pursue other interests off the track, knowing it would only enhance his ability to win races. This partnership will go down in history as the most successful ever. Lewis has always referred to Mercedes as his family, and having him there as a driver has raised the profile of the team. Whether he would have retired whilst at the top if he had won the championship in 2021, we will never know.

It was at the end of 2021 that certain fans started to turn against Mercedes, accusing them of not taking Red Bull to court and suing them for robbing Lewis on the last lap by changing the rules to suit themselves. But Toto Wolff did take advice about this, and was told that a court would simply cancel that last race, and Verstappen would still win because, although they were equal on points, Verstappen had won one more race than Lewis. Lewis himself insisted that he didn't want to win a championship in a courtroom, so out of respect for him, Toto Wolff did not proceed any further. There were other possible repercussions too, as Mercedes filing a complaint against the FIA could result in a long and involved litigation trial, and the possibilities of team AMG MERCEDES being the losers, and forced out of the FIA.

Then, in 2022, everything came crashing down for Mercedes. They struggled with the new regulations, which had been introduced to help other teams, and the car they produced was not competitive. Lewis made it his mission to try and help the team that had given him so much support and enabled him to achieve seven championships. He did this at the expense of losing championship points; he liaised with the team to try and improve the car, not only for himself, but for his team mate Russell.

After two years of being unable to win any races, he was being courted by Ferrari, and he made the monumental decision to join them in 2025. He knew his time for racing was running out, and he wanted to win that elusive eighth championship. Toto had wanted him to win that championship with Mercedes, but he knew the car was still not competitive in 2024.

It was a huge blow to Mercedes to lose Sir Lewis Hamilton, which was why they were not rushing to sign anyone. His worth to the team, whether he won or lost races was huge, but Toto has wished him well, and stated that if Ferrari can give him a competitive car, he can win that championship.

Nobody knows how many years Lewis will drive for Ferrari, his deal is for three, but it could be more. They are certainly welcoming him with open arms, but no matter what, he will always think of Mercedes as his family. Those fans that angrily berate Mercedes for not giving him a fast car should remember his own words: 'We win and lose together.'

Lewis still has so much love and respect for Mercedes, and so should the fans. Without Mercedes his championship tally would not be seven. If he doesn't win the moment he steps into the Ferrari car, will they hurl abuse at them? They are very protective of him, so this could certainly happen. Fans are there to support their driver and his team, so hopefully Lewis was able to enjoy his last season with Mercedes.

13

Canada

In the past Canada had been a great circuit for Lewis Hamilton, having won there seven times. His first win was in 2007, when, as a rookie, against double world champion Alonso, he claimed his first victory. Before this year's race, a post was put up on his Instagram account reminiscing about how special it had felt when he won his first race.

At the press conference on Thursday, Lewis was asked whether the updates on the car might bring Mercedes nearer to a podium finish, and he agreed that hopefully they might not be too far away. He now also had the new wing that Russell ran at the last race.

In the practice sessions Lewis was flying, his pace was great, and all the fans were holding their breath in anticipation, wondering if this form could carry through to qualifying. During the first part of qualifying Mercedes were 1st and 2nd, and Russell managed to carry that through to Q3, he then got a tow from Albon which helped him to get pole position.

But Lewis was not so lucky. When he did his push lap in Q3, the wind had got up, and he made an error. Once again, with such small margins between the drivers, he ended up in 7th. He was very despondent when interviewed afterwards, saying he had no idea why when he gets to Q3 he seems to lose two tenths. But in spite of his disappointment, he was quick to congratulate George on his pole position.

On race day, conditions were mixed, the track was wet as it had been raining, and when the drivers set off spray was going everywhere. It was an eventful race with four safety cars, and the lead of the race changed several times. It did look as if Norris would win it at one time, but he opted not to come in under the safety car, so when he did pit, he had to relinquish his lead for 2nd place. Russell was overtaken by Norris and Verstappen, who ended up winning it. Norris was 2nd, Russell 3rd, and a valiant effort from Lewis saw him rise up to 4th place, making up three places from where he started the race. Russell was delighted to be on the podium, even though he had not won, but Lewis, as always very self critical, declared it was his worst race for a long time. What frustrated him was the fact he felt if he had qualified better, he could have won the race. He made a comment about getting his head together to qualify higher. The fact that he came 4th, his highest result during the year so far, did not satisfy him, but for the fans it was a positive. It meant that Mercedes had definitely improved their car, and with the British Grand Prix coming up in July, and three British drivers in contention, it would make a very exciting race. Although Verstappen did prevail, the gap was closing, so the second part of the season was set to be an exciting time.

14

Spain

Sir Lewis Hamilton has a diverse range of interests outside Formula One. He has always loved movies, and is now producing his own movie about Formula One, which stars Brad Pitt and Damson Idris. Production had been held up because of a strike, but it was announced before the Spanish Grand Prix that it will be released in June 2025.

Many of the scenes were filmed at Silverstone during a grand prix weekend, as Lewis was anxious to make it as authentic as possible. Brad Pitt plays a retired Formula One driver, who returns to drive in a team, and Damson Idris plays his team mate. When the film crew arrived to shoot the scenes, the other drivers seemed to enjoy the experience of having them there, and the FIA willingly gave their permission for it to proceed. News about the release date of the movie quickly spread around the paddock, and it is expected to prove very popular with the fans.

During the week before the Spanish Grand Prix, news broke that an email had been circulating within the F1 community accusing Mercedes of sabotaging Lewis Hamilton's efforts in 2024. It mentioned his tyres, and his position within the team, and also stated that it was affecting his mental health. It is quite clear to any normal fan that no team would ever sabotage their driver, as they want to get as many points as they can, so it was definitely not in their interest to do this. They also accused Mercedes of favouring Russell, but it was understandable, with Lewis departing at the end of the year to go to Ferrari, and George staying on, they would have no choice but to exclude him from meetings later on so that he did not have knowledge of any data that would help another team.

Toto Wolff was extremely angry about this email and the allegations. He has always held Lewis in high regard, both as a work colleague and a friend, so his response was to call the police in to try and work out who the perpetrator was. It had stated that the person was a member of the Mercedes team, which has been proved to be untrue, but whoever it was, they were clearly paranoid, and one would hope that true fans of Lewis would not even give such comments any credibility. Lewis himself called for unity, asking the fans to unite to give Mercedes the support they needed, and he completely refuted all the claims.

Before the race had even started, there was even more drama happening off the track, as the McLaren headquarters suffered a fire. Luckily no one was seriously hurt, and when interviewed afterwards, Team Principal Zak Brown spoke about how the FIA and other teams and members had rallied round to help them in their hour of need.

It was believed that the Spanish circuit would suit Red Bull more than the bumpy tracks had, so they were expected to once again be dominant and beat all other teams. Mercedes were not

Lewis Fan Photographs

From top left: Molly Willoughby, Bex Guest, Group Photo taken by Bex Guest, Alex and Poppy Lurring, Renáta Szabó.

sure whether their improvements, which worked with the Canadian circuit, would also put them further up the order on the Spanish track.

Practice 1 was uneventful with Russell finishing P4 and Lewis P7. But in practice 2 Lewis led the way, posting the fastest lap of anybody. By the time they reached qualifying, he was stating how nice the car was to drive, and it appeared his confidence in it was growing.

After a very tight qualifying, Norris took a brilliant pole, and Verstappen was 2nd. Lewis came 3rd, his best qualifying position since 2021, and Russell, who was very close, was 4th. Verstappen had a tow from Perez, and Russell also had a tow, which is usually worth at least a couple of tenths of time, but it did not help either of them to improve their position.

Lewis was in a very buoyant mood after his highest qualifying for such a long time, and he credited the team with all the hard work they had been doing to improve the car. He vowed to do his utmost to try and win on Sunday, and said he hoped that he could work with Russell to attack the cars in front.

On race day it was bright and sunny for the start of the race. Lewis had a bad start, he said he lost power briefly, and meanwhile Russell flew off the line, and then got a slipstream from Verstappen and Norris, which propelled him into 1st place. Lewis was almost swallowed up by the Ferraris behind, but just managed to hang onto 4th place. A lap later, Verstappen overtook Russell. Norris was behind him, but after pitting he managed to gain a one second lap faster, and Russell dropped to 3rd place.

There were no safety cars in the race, so it all came down to tyre wear. When Russell went in for his 2nd pit stop, he was given hard tyres because he had already worn his soft tyres out. Lewis pitted on lap 44 for soft tyres, after overtaking Sainz he set his sights on his team mate, and after overtaking him, he pulled out a lead of over five seconds on him, and claimed the final place on the podium.

Apart from his runner up position in China, this was his first finish on the podium for 2024. His face was wreathed in smiles, and the cheers from the fans were loud. He thanked them all for their support, and also his team for all the hard work they had put in to improve the car.

Mercedes stated that they intended to keep adding updates on the car, and Lewis said how much nicer the car was to drive, and how they really hoped to keep improving. His aim, of course, was to finish on the top of the podium before leaving Mercedes.

15

Austria

It was only one week after Spain that the Austrian Grand Prix would take place, and one week after that the Great Britain race at Silverstone. During the week before, it was announced that the police had done their investigation into the person who had sent the email accusing Mercedes of sabotaging Lewis Hamilton. The conclusion was that no actual crime had been committed, and it appeared to have been sent by one of his fans. It was sad to think that someone would go to those lengths, but it showed how seriously Toto Wolff had taken it, and his desire to protect Lewis and his team by calling in the police.

During sprint weekend, only one practice is allowed before sprint qualifying, and it's absolutely imperative to get the car set up correctly. During practice Lewis looked more comfortable in the car than he has for a while, and he ran hard tyres whilst others were on soft.

But his euphoria was short-lived, because in qualifying Russell came 4th and Lewis was 6th. Afterwards Russell felt he could get onto the podium, but as always Lewis was very self critical, stating that his laps were messy. The sprint race turned out to be uneventful, except for one exciting moment, when 2nd placed Norris briefly overtook pole sitter Verstappen. This gave Piastri a chance to take 2nd position, meanwhile Verstappen won the race and Russell came 4th after getting past Sainz who had overtaken him at the start. Lewis was stuck in 6th and unable to make headway, even though he was running very close to Sainz.

Later in the day, when qualifying for the main race took place, it was commented on how low Lewis's car was running, and sparks were flying. Both Mercedes drivers got through to Q3, qualifying 4th for Russell and 6th for Lewis. However, Oscar Piastri had his lap deleted because he exceeded track limits, which cost him a grid penalty, so he dropped to 7th, which elevated Lewis to 5th and Russell to 3rd.

On race day the weather was sunny, Lewis lost no time in passing Sainz for 4th place, and then he passed his team mate for 3rd, but Russell came back and regained the place. His overtake on Sainz had caused him to leave the track, which meant he had to give the place back to avoid a ten second penalty, which he did. He also sustained floor damage, which was to affect his pace for the rest of the race.

It certainly was not Lewis's day, as later, when taking a pit stop, he was fractionally over the pit lane line. Piastri reported him, and when the stewards looked at it, they decided to give him a five second penalty. Toto came on the radio to encourage him, which was nice to hear .

Meanwhile, up at the front, after a slow pit stop, which cost Verstappen valuable time, he found himself being pursued by Norris for first place. Their battle on track became very feisty, with stewards noting their misdemeanours. Then Verstappen defended hard against Norris, pushing him off the track and causing a puncture, which ultimately ended his race. Verstappen was given a ten second time penalty.

All of a sudden George Russell had a chance of a win, with both cars in front out of the running. Verstappen's penalty dropped him down to 5th place. So Russell took his 2nd win, Piastri was 2nd, Sainz was 3rd. and Lewis was 4th.

Afterwards Lewis showed his class by congratulating George on his win, and said he was delighted for the team that they had their first win of 2024. He criticised himself for having 'A poor race,' although it was nice to see that as a team they had picked up some valuable points between them. Verstappen and Norris both blamed each other. It was, however, commented on by many people that, now his car was not so dominant, Verstappen cracked under pressure; and if he thought he was losing, he would push his opponent off, rather than race fairly. He did this to Lewis all through 2021, and mostly went unpunished by the FIA. Instead of advising him to race fairly, Horner made it worse by trying to blame Norris, so Verstappen saw no fault in himself, and no doubt would carry on defending in the same reckless way.

The following weekend was the British Grand Prix, and we had three British drivers, all anxious to win, or at least get on the podium. In the past Lewis had won so many times that 'The Hamilton Strait' has been named after him in recognition of his seven titles and record wins. No wonder his home Grand Prix is so special to him. The fans were wishing him well for the following week.

16

The British Grand Prix

During the week leading up to the British Grand Prix, it was announced by the BBC that Lewis Hamilton would be appearing on CBeebies Bedtime Stories on 3rd July 2024 to share that no dream is too big. He explains in a short video that nothing is impossible if you can set your mind to it and everyone can dream big and challenge oneself.

Sir Lewis has always shown great kindness to the children who support him at the race track, and many parents with sick children have reached out to him over the years, at which time he has responded by meeting those children, knowing how much it meant to them. There is no doubt that his video will have been very inspiring and exciting for the CBeebies audience.

By the time Wednesday of the British Grand Prix week had arrived, the internet was alight with articles condemning Verstappen for 'racing unfairly, and deliberately taking Norris out rather than lose to him in Austria.' Red Bull and Horner reacted by saying, 'This is the way Max races; he will never

d

give in because he is a tough racer, and he has done nothing wrong. It was Norris's fault.'

No matter which side the fans are on, it seemed the stewards had definitely decided that Verstappen was at fault because a ten second penalty was apparently the maximum punishment he could have had, and did have, plus two points on his super licence.

McLaren team principal Andrea Stella went as far as to question Horner's integrity following the clash between the two drivers which forced Norris to retire. Verstappen went on to claim 5th place after a penalty, and to extend his championship lead. Horner stated that Norris was trying to cause something to happen up at turn three, which Stella was most unhappy to hear. His reply was to the effect that he thought this kind of statement was pretty annoying, and that to some extent it speaks for the integrity of the person who made it.

Andreas had previously remarked that Verstappen's aggressive driving during 2021 against Lewis Hamilton was never punished properly, which was why he still did it when challenged by another driver. For the past two years, whilst Red Bull has been so dominant, he had driven alone and unchallenged, but now he had others who were matching him with a fast car, he had reverted back to his old driving habits.

Obviously, as far as Mercedes was concerned, the tussle between those two drivers gave Russell the opportunity to win the race in the previous week, but now the fans were on the edge of their seats to see if it happened again at Silverstone.

During the driver's conference on Thursday, Lewis was asked if he agreed with Stella's remarks about Verstappen, but he refused to be drawn, saying it was nothing to do with him. He was also asked if he could teach Norris how to defend against Verstappen, but again, declined to be drawn, saying that Norris didn't need lessons about defending from him.

In the meantime, Norris had apparently cooled down, and said Verstappen had no need to apologise to him and everything was now good between them again. Drivers sometimes react angrily in the heat of the moment; or alternatively, it may be that diplomacy was needed with the British race coming up so soon afterwards. So harmony had been restored, but fans would be watching both of them if they were anywhere near each other on the grid.

The weather forecast was for varying conditions during the Silverstone weekend, which was exciting news for the fans. It meant that it would be more down to drivers' skill in mastering the track, rather than being in the fastest car.

Mercedes looked fairly strong in practice, and Lewis and George both said they felt comfortable in the car. In qualifying in changeable conditions, which seemed to fare well for Mercedes, it was exciting. Lewis led the time sheets in Q1 and Q2, but in Q3, Russell beat him by a tenth to claim pole, and Lewis was 2nd.

Lewis praised George and the team for their endeavours, but as always he was criticised by the media. David Coulthard on Channel 4, questioned that maybe 'Lewis in his prime would not have been beaten to pole.' There had been tales circulating for a while now that Lewis was no longer the racer that he was, and why would he go to Ferrari and not retire? Armchair critics find it easy to try and bring someone so successful down, but the fans of Lewis were actually quite excited that he would be starting the race from the first row.

Race day was sunny at the beginning, but was to turn out to

be a day of mixed conditions. Opinions of who would win the race varied between Verstappen, who was starting 4th, Norris who was 3rd, Russell who was on pole, and very few, apart from his own loyal fans, actually thought Lewis could do it, because he hadn't won a race for two and a half years. Betting odds only put Lewis as maybe finishing on the podium.

Lewis had already said that he could work with Russell to keep the other cars behind, so they could win the race. They both got a good start, and Lewis positioned his car to stop Verstappen and Norris from overtaking him or George, and initially they were able to pull away. A few laps later, when the rain started, Lewis overtook Russell. With conditions changing all the time, it became apparent they were on the wrong tyres, as they were both overtaken by Verstappen, Norris and Piastri.

Mercedes called them in for a double stack pit stop, which was executed to perfection, and in the meantime Piastri had also pitted. Following Norris's pit stop, Lewis was just passing the pit entrance, and he managed to get himself ahead of him into 1st place. He now had to make sure his tyres would last him until the end of the race. Sadly for Russell, his car had to be retired for a hydraulic leak, which must have been very disappointing for him at his home grand prix. It was now up to Lewis to get Mercedes a good result.

During those last few laps, he just kept going. The spectators were cheering him all the way round, the atmosphere was electric, and all the while, Verstappen, in the faster car, was catching him. But by lap 52, Verstappen had to settle for 2nd place, being just over a second behind him. He had overtaken Norris, who was now 3rd, and Lewis now had his 9th win at Silverstone, and was referred to as the King of Silverstone. The crowd went wild with excitement. This was the man, who after being deprived of his eighth title, then spent two and a half years trying to help his team get back to where they should be. He never gave up, had won again, and what better place than his home Grand Prix!

The emotion when he got out of the car was shared by everyone; tears of joy. Bono, his race engineer, declared: 'I wouldn't say tears, just something in my eye.' Anthony, the man who had guided his son on this spectacular journey in F1, was there to hug him, as was his beautiful mother Carmen. Lewis drove around the track with the Union Jack, acknowledging the fans, then he ran around the grass on the circuit holding the Union Jack flag up, nobody does it better than he does, and the crowd roared with appreciation.

If anyone had any doubts whether Sir Lewis Hamilton had 'still got it' the answer was right there. For all the trolls and fair weather fans who had hurled insults at Mercedes, accusing them of sabotaging him, and for the neurotic fan who sent the email, this was their answer. He was not done yet!

17

Euphoria

After the British Grand Prix, the joy from the fans that the race had been won by a Briton was euphoric. Sir Lewis Hamilton, the man who had been written off by some as 'too old' or 'past his prime', along with many other derogatory comments, had proved them all wrong. The fact that he had continued for two and a half years to train, compete, and believe he could win again was so uplifting to many. He was hailed as an inspiration, and even fans of McLaren and Red Bull praised him for mastering the changing conditions and winning the race in a car which was not the fastest on the grid .

Fans suddenly starting praising Mercedes again. Indeed that praise was well deserved, as their excellent execution of a double stack pit stop, and the feedback from Lewis about the track and when he should come in, had been instrumental in sealing the win. During the final laps, when it looked like Verstappen was closing on Lewis, the fans cheered Lewis all the way round, some even losing their voice in their excitement.

Celebrations continued; Lewis was shedding tears of relief after such a long drought, and the fans cried with him. Pundits were calling him the GOAT once again. In winning this race at

Silverstone he had now reached a new record of 104 wins, broken the record as the oldest driver to win a Grand Prix, set a new record as the only driver to win again 17 years after his first win and another record winning after 300 starts. The excitement and relief at this result affected everyone. Toto Wolff remarked that it was like a fairytale for Lewis to win the British Grand Prix during his last season with the team.

Fred Vasseur of Ferrari praised Lewis, commenting how delighted he was that Lewis would be joining them in 2025, as he felt his input and motivation would help the team to improve. David Coulthard had to eat his words and acknowledge what a great drive Lewis had done in very difficult circumstances, and Mark Webber, a retired Red Bull driver, declared he was a huge Hamilton fan, stating that not only was he a huge inspiration on the track, but his work in inclusivity, making the USA aware of Formula One, and all the other work he has done to enhance the sport deserves more recognition because 'Lewis Hamilton is Formula One.'

Silverstone always puts on a great show during the Formula One weekend. The weather can be very unpredictable, and kudos to the fans who sat there in the pouring rain at times, toughing it out to see their favourite drivers. The fact that it was a British driver, and the one who holds all the records, only added to the excitement. Silverstone really took Lewis Hamilton to their hearts that day. Seeing him win again, and how much it meant to him touched everyone.

The following weekend would be the Hungarian Grand Prix, where in the past Lewis had won eight times and also gained eight pole positions. The burning questions on the lips of his fans were: Could he win again? Had the car been improved enough to run at the front of the grid?

18

Hungary

During the week running up to the Hungarian Grand Prix, it was announced that Sir Lewis Hamilton was now an ambassador for Dior, and that this partnership would see him debut his own fashion collection in October 2024. Because he is vegan, Sir Lewis has ensured that his sneaker and clothing capsule collection is crafted from vegan materials, inspired by winter sports such as skiing and snowboarding.

In the same week it was also announced that Sir Lewis Hamilton had been voted the greatest British athlete of the 21st century, and a trophy was presented to him. He had some stiff competition, with the likes of Sir Andy Murray, Dame Laura Kenney and Sir Chris Hoy, to name just a few. It was reported that Sir Lewis was surprised and delighted to be presented with the trophy, and extremely humble in his response.

The weather in Hungary was extremely hot during practice 1 and 2, with hotter temperatures promised for race day. The track could reach temperatures as high as fifty degrees. The Mercedes car struggles on hot tracks, and after the session, Lewis explained that it had not been easy, but running had allowed them to collect useful data to try and help the car perform better in the hot conditions. Both Lewis and George had been very motivated during the press sessions, declaring that they intended to push as much as they could to try and get some more wins before the end of the season.

During qualifying, conditions were cooler for Q1, which allowed Lewis to top the time sheets. But by the time they got to Q3, it had become hotter. Lewis just made it into the top ten, and then he did his flying lap, which put him into 5th place. McLaren were 1st and 2nd, with Norris on pole, and Verstappen, who was visibly frustrated, in 3rd. Then came Sainz before Lewis in 5th.

Russell did not make it out of Q1, and was unable to run again because of lack of fuel. So he had to settle for 17th position.

On race day, the weather was hot. Lewis made a good start, which put him past Sainz and up to 4th. Meanwhile Verstappen passed Norris, but had to give the position back because he had gained an advantage when he went off track. Russell set himself the task of trying to climb up into the points. By the end of the race he had made it to eighth place.

Lewis pitted early on lap 17 for hard tyres, which undercut Verstappen, who was visibly frustrated, and during the race he became angry, berating his team over the radio for what he felt was a bad strategy. He made two attempts to overtake Lewis and claim 3rd place. The first time he went off the track, and the second time he dived down the side of Lewis and hit his car. Luckily neither of them, nor their cars, suffered any damage. Verstappen's car actually lifted up into the air for a moment, and when he managed to straighten up again, he had lost another place to Leclerc.so ended up 5th. The stewards looked at it after the race and decided it was a racing incident, so no penalties were applied. Piastri won and Norris was 2nd, after McLaren had swapped them around at the end of the race due to a pit stop undercut.

Lewis's drive was hailed as a masterclass in defending, as he had spent most of the race fending off Verstappen in the quicker car. When he reached the chequered flag, Bono, his engineer, came on the radio to congratulate him, and to point out it was his 200th podium; another record that nobody else has accomplished.

Finally Lewis's season was improving rapidly. With his new haul of points, he had come from eighth place in the Drivers' Championship to sixth. He was now in a much better place mentally.

19

Belgium

After the last two races, where he made it onto the podium, Lewis Hamilton was excited to get to Belgium. The track at Spa is one he likes a lot, having won there five times in the past. But during practice both Lewis and Russell found their cars very hard to drive, and so the engineers decided to take the updates off the car, and revert to the settings from the British Grand Prix. Later Andrew Shovlin found out what the problem was, so they went into qualifying not really knowing what to expect.

Verstappen had a new engine, so would be taking a ten pace grid penalty for exceeding his quota. He was very fast in qualifying, which had wet conditions, and easily achieved pole by six tenths of a second. Lewis came 4th, Leclerc was 2nd, and Perez 3rd, with Russell 7th. This meant Verstappen would start in 11th position, and they all moved up a place, which made Lewis 3rd.

He stated afterwards that it would be a tough race, with Red Bull and Ferrari faster. To make the podium would be difficult, but as always, he promised to give his all. Pundits suggested that, with the raw pace that the new engine was showing, Verstappen would quickly make his way to the front.

Race day was warm and sunny, but not too hot, which was always better for Mercedes. Lewis made a great start, immediately overtaking Perez. A couple of laps later he had passed Leclerc, and clearly meant business. He held the lead and controlled the race.

Verstappen struggled to make headway, which surprised everyone, and seemed to be continually stuck in a DRS (drag reduction system) train. Lewis had a good pit stop, and changed to hard tyres from medium. The fast McLaren's didn't seem to be making inroads either, which was a huge surprise, as Spa is a track where drivers are usually able to overtake.

After his first pit stop, Lewis still held the lead of the race, and then he was called in for another pit stop, some 16 laps before the end of the race. He told his race engineer that his tyres were still good, but he was still advised to pit, and he did so, because he has complete faith in their ability to give him the best strategy to win the race. Then Russell was told to 'box box', but he stated that he was staying out. He was at that time running 1st because everyone else including Lewis had pitted. The team conceded that he could stay out, although Lewis did not know until later that Russell had not pitted. Some laps later, Russell was asked again if he wanted to pit, but he insisted he wanted to stay out, so the team went with his decision.

Bono told Lewis about Russell, and Lewis then asked if he had enough laps left to catch him on his newer tyres. Bono said he could, but it would be close. So Lewis set himself the task of catching him up, and he managed to get up to two tenths behind him, but was unable to pass because of the dirty air.

In the meantime, Piastri was closing on Lewis, and it was expected that there would be team orders to stop Lewis, who was much faster than Russell, falling into the clutches of Piastri, and losing his position.

But team orders never came. Russell won, Lewis was 2nd, and he just managed to hold off Piastri by less than a second, who was 3rd. Russell was jubilant, and Lewis did congratulate him, but his body language told a different story. He explained in his interview that he had also told his engineer his tyres were good, but taken the advice given that it was better to pit.

Within two hours, it was announced that Russell had been disqualified because his car was too light, apparently only doing one stop had worn his tyres down too much, and there was also a problem with the fuel. By running so much lighter, he had a huge advantage over the other cars, and it made him much faster. This meant Lewis was the winner, Piastri now 2nd, and Leclerc 3rd.

Lewis released a statement later to say how sorry he was that George had been disqualified, as it wasn't the way he liked to win, but the positive to take from it was they were heading into the summer break with a much improved car. The team apologised to Russell, and said they would look into the weight problem and learn from it. Russell took a chance by questioning the strategy; if he had pitted, it was believed he would have come 5th with 10 points, but sadly for him, being disqualified meant he lost all his points.

The season was getting much more exciting, with battles between different drivers in every race now. Red Bull had slipped away again, with Verstappen taking 5th and Perez 8th. There would now be a month's break, but every team wanted to come back stronger.

PART TWO

20

Zandvoort

By the time the August Bank holiday weekend came round, Formula One fans were more than ready for the season to continue. Now that it appeared that other teams had caught up with Red Bull, it was hard to know who would win the races. With so many teams fighting for supremacy, it made it all much more exciting.

Now that Mercedes had improved the car, both the drivers were excited to get back to fighting the other teams. Lewis had found more confidence since his epic Silverstone win, and stated that he couldn't wait to get back in the car.

During practice, they found their pace to be good, and with changing weather conditions in qualifying, they were aiming to compete for pole. Russell struggled for grip in P1, but Lewis managed to top the sheets. But in Q2, Lewis suffered with a lack of grip, which saw him fail to get through to Q3, and end up in 12th. Sainz also suffered, and was 11th. Norris got pole, Verstappen 2nd, Piastri 3rd, and Russell 4th. Lewis was downbeat afterwards, not really understanding what had gone wrong, but knowing that on Sunday it would be all about fighting back, and trying to move up the order.

Later Lewis's situation became worse, as he was summoned by the stewards for impeding Perez, and was given a three place grid drop. He would have started 15th, but then Albon was disqualified for having an illegal floor, which moved him up to 14th.

The weather was dry for the race, and when it started, Verstappen jumped Norris to take the lead. Russell overtook Piastri for 3rd, and Lewis, on soft tyres, set to work to move himself up the grid. He made up six places to 8th, and then pitted for hard tyres. He came out in 14th, and had to do it all again. Russell was overtaken by Piastri, and then due to excessive tyre wear, had to pit twice more, so he ended up in 7th. Lewis caught up with him by the end of the race, but kept behind.

When interviewed afterwards, Lewis rued his poor qualifying, and stated that if he had qualified higher up, he could have done a better job, and maybe even got on the podium.

Russell complained that the car had no grip, and the tyre wear was excessive. Toto Wolff was very downbeat, saying after the recent wins, 7th and 8th places were very disappointing, and he promised the team would look into the data to try and understand what went wrong.

Norris took a dominant win after passing Verstappen, some 22 seconds ahead, Verstappen was 2nd, and Leclerc did an excellent race, after qualifying in 6th, and finishing 3rd.

The Italian Grand Prix was just one week away, and Lewis hoped to do well in front of the Tifosi, as they would be his new fan base in the following year.

21

Italy

The Tifosi are very passionate fans, and for their home race they would want Ferrari to win. The Mercedes' team made an upgrade to the car, hoping it would give them a chance to fight McLaren, which appeared to have the fastest car right now.

Just before the Italian Grand Prix, Toto Wolff put Kimi Antonelli into Russell's car for a trial run in practice 1. His first lap was scorchingly fast, but on the 2nd lap, he lost control of the car, and crashed into the barriers. Luckily he was unhurt, but many Formula One fans mocked him on social media, and it makes one wonder how good these armchair critics would be if they were in his place.

Undeterred by this, shortly afterwards Toto Wolff announced that in 2025 Kimi would be taking the seat left vacant by Lewis Hamilton. Kimi also released a statement saying that nobody could replace Lewis Hamilton, and he was honoured to be in the Mercedes team next year. Lewis himself became emotional, stating how much he loved the Mercedes team, the history they had created together, and nothing would change that. Toto Wolff published a statement which left nobody in any doubt about how important Lewis had been to them.

"The Mercedes team just love Lewis Hamilton, and will continue to love him whether he is in a red overall or doing something else, he'll always be part of this family."

Lewis felt very comfortable in his car during practice, and topped the time sheets in Q3. He was eagerly looking forward to qualifying. Indeed it was all looking good in qualifying, but in Q3, once again, it went wrong for him, by thousandths of a seconds, he ended up 6th. Lewis is always self critical, and he was very angry with himself, as he had believed he could have made pole. Norris was pole, Piastri 2nd and Russell 3rd. Leclerc was 4th, Sainz 5th and Lewis 6th.

Lewis was clearly feeling vulnerable, as he said he hoped Kimi could do a better job for the team next year, as he felt he had let them down. Mercedes responded by saying Lewis was the best qualifier ever, his records proved that, and he would be even better in the race the following day.

The weather was very hot on race day, which does not really suit the Mercedes car. At the start, Lewis was fast off the line, and gained a position to 5th. Russell hit a bollard after narrowly avoiding Piastri, which left his end plate hanging, and sent him down to 8th place. After a while he pitted, and got a new part and fresh tyres. When Lewis pitted he came out in 10th and worked his way up the grid again to 5th. In the meantime, Piastri had overtaken Norris, and was leading the race. But the McLarens had to pit again because of tyre wear, whereas Leclerc managed a one stop, and was able to win the race. It was an excellent drive by him, and the Tifosi were ecstatic with happiness. Sainz was 4th, just ahead of Lewis, who also had to make two stops, and Russell was 7th.

Verstappen was 6th and Perez 8th, and now McLaren are just a few points behind them in the Constructors' Championship.

Verstappen's lead in the championship has been slashed to 62 points, although with so few races left, it's unlikely anyone can challenge him.

Mercedes conceded that their pace had not been there, and they needed to look into why that was. They had two weeks until the next race to try and improve the car.

22

Baku

After originally believing that outgoing car designer from Red Bull, Adrian Newey, might join forces with Lewis at Ferrari in 2025, rumours abounded that Lawrence Stroll from Aston Martin was offering him a blank cheque, along with a partnership. Newey would also be allowed to bring his own team of engineers in.

Speculation continued for some time. Fred Vasseur confirmed that negotiations had fallen through, and Ferrari did not wish to meet the demands of Newey. On Tuesday 10th September it was officially announced that Newey would join Aston Martin in the spring of 2025. Fans of Lewis had mixed emotions about this. Some were disappointed, whereas others pointed out that Lewis had won all of his seven titles without the input of Newey. Lewis did not pass any comment, other than stating that with only a short time left with Mercedes, he wants to finish his time there on a high.

The last two races since the second half of the season started had not been as competitive as the previous few before the break, but Mercedes had worked hard to try and understand the drop in performance. Toto announced that they had looked into this, and hopefully the car would perform better, as they wanted to earn as many championship points as possible.

On press day, inevitably Lewis was asked how he felt about Adrian Newey going to Aston Martin, and he explained that obviously it would have been very nice to have worked with him, but that he was only one man, and there was a team of engineers involved. He also said it changed nothing, as his focus was to help Ferrari in 2025, who as a team had been unable to challenge for a championship for many years, and all his energy would be spent doing that.

In 1st practice, Lewis came 2nd to Verstappen with Russell 8th, and in practice 2 he was 3rd, with Leclerc and Perez ahead of him. Clearly their car had had some improvements made to it. Russell was 9th, although no doubt he would be a lot higher in qualifying.

As expected, in qualifying, the tyre problems in Q3 came back to haunt Lewis. This man was the person with the highest amount of pole positions in Formula One history, but this year he could not get his tyres to work in Q3, which was so frustrating for him. He ended up qualifying 7th, Russell was 5th, as he also struggled. Charles Leclerc gained a fine pole, with Piastri 2nd and Sainz 3rd. Verstappen was 6th.

It was announced in the morning before the race that Lewis had taken a new engine, so would start the race from the pit lane, which meant he would have to fight his way up to the top ten to try for points. Lewis was optimistic that changes had been made to the car to help in this.

When the race started, Leclerc led to Piastri, then Sainz and Perez. Russell initially was overtaken by Verstappen, but later in the race, was able to get his position back. Lewis found his car completely lacking pace, and balance, so was really struggling to make headway. In the meantime, the first three were very close to one another, and eventually Leclerc was overtaken by Piastri. The gap was very close, but Leclerc was unable to retake his position, whereas Perez was looking strong. But an incident between Perez and Sainz took them both out of the race towards the end, which elevated Russell to 3rd on the podium. Norris, who had failed to get out of Q1 in qualifying, had managed to get himself up to 4th position, and Verstappen was 5th.

Lewis ended up 9th, earning two points, but his struggle with the car showed that since the summer break Mercedes had taken a step back, which was disappointing for all the team.

The following week, racing resumed in Singapore, so whether Mercedes could sort out why their car was once again so difficult to drive in such a short time was unknown.

Russell was grateful to finish 3rd because of Perez and Sainz not finishing; he did remark over the radio, when he crossed the line, 'Tyres, tyres.'

Verstappen's lead over Norris in the championship now stood at 59 points.

23

Singapore

During the week leading up to the Singapore Grand Prix, it was announced by the FIA that they would be stamping down on bad language, and punish any of the drivers that used it, as it was felt, although some of the radio calls were bleeped out, that it was not a good look for Formula One.

The first person to fall foul of the new rule was Verstappen, who used the 'F' word whilst describing his car during a conversation at the driver's press conference. He was duly summoned to the stewards, who decided that as a punishment he should do some sort of charitable work, for them to be able to draw a line under it. Many within the paddock were amused by this new rule, as Verstappen is well known for his expletive rants, especially when his car is not performing how he wants it to. His angry retort was:

"Surely we are not five year olds."

Both Lewis and Russell really struggled with their cars in all practices. The balance was wrong, and the team of Mercedes' engineers worked tirelessly to try and improve it for them.

Lewis gloomily remarked that unless a solution could be found, they would really struggle in qualifying. In the past he had never qualified outside the top five at this track, and had won on four previous occasions.

It was a tense qualifying session, and towards the end Sainz put his car into the wall, bringing out a red flag, but luckily he was unhurt. After a restart, in which everyone had just one lap to post a time, he and Leclerc made up the last two in the top ten. Lewis was surprised to find his car 'come alive', as he put it. By the end of Q3 Lewis found himself in 3rd, narrowly beaten by Verstappen, who was 2nd. Norris took pole position by a good margin. Russell was 4th and Piastri 5th. When interviewed after, Lewis explained that his car had felt good in qualifying, and this had not happened to him for a long time. The tyres were in the right window, and the relief in his voice was evident, as he had spent all of this season trying to qualify better than he had, not understanding what was going wrong. He knew that starting on the second row gave him a chance to fight for a position on the podium.

Even though the race at Marina Bray is held at night, it was still extremely humid, and this time was no exception. It was noted at the beginning, that Lewis was on soft tyres, whereas most of the other drivers, except Ricciardo, were on mediums. Knowing how good Lewis is usually at preserving his tyres, Mercedes were hoping the faster tyre might give him a higher track position. Indeed, at the start, he attempted to overtake Verstappen for 3rd, but the Dutch man held him off. It wasn't long before Lewis and the team realised the soft tyres were not going to work, and he would be forced to make an early stop to change the tyres. After he had stopped, he pointed this out to Bono, and was clearly not happy.

Lewis came out in 13th place after his stop, with much work to do to get back into the top ten. He bravely fought his way back to 6th place, and Russell managed to keep his 4th place. The tyre strategy had ruined any chance Lewis had of making the podium. Norris won, with Verstappen 2nd and Piastri 3rd.

There was much speculation when Toto announced that Lewis and Russell would not be at the press conference afterwards as they were both suffering from heatstroke. Many fans had slated Mercedes for ruining Lewis's race, and in their eyes 'favouring Russell'. No doubt Lewis would have had strong words about his tyre strategy, but later Toto and Bono both issued an apology to Lewis, admitting the team had messed up badly.

Later, Lewis himself issued a message: 'It's hard to describe the emotions after a race like that. We don't always get things right, and that was the case today with our strategy, but we'll come together, analyse and refocus for Austin.'

Lewis had already moved on, because he knew it was the only thing to do. It was now four weeks until the next race in Austin, which gave everyone a chance to regroup and for the drivers to recharge their batteries.

It was reported that Lewis and Russell were both fine now, after soaking in a bathtub full of ice cubes. That was the best news the fans could possibly hear.

24

Events Before Austin

Before the race in Singapore took place, rumours had abounded that Red Bull were going to take Ricciardo out of the V CARB team and replace him with Liam Lawson. Normally changes happen at the end of the season, but Red Bull always seem to have their own rules.

Daniel Ricciardo joined Formula One in 2011, at the age of 21. During that time he has achieved 8 race wins, 3 pole positions, 17 fastest laps, and 32 podium positions. At one time it was believed he would be a future world champion, but when he struggled whilst at McLaren in 2023 he was replaced by Oscar Piastri, and moved into Red Bull's secondary team V CARB.

At the Singapore race he had a good drive, and claimed a point for the fastest lap. Fans responded by voting him Driver of the Day. But it was not until the race was over that Red Bull officially announced that his place was going to be taken by Lawson, and that had, in fact, been his last race.

Normally when a driver leaves after such a long career, there are celebrations, testimonials from other drivers, doughnuts being performed in race cars, and partying, but all this poor man

e

was greeted with when he left the track was emptiness, because nobody realised the rumour was true, and they all went home.

It was really hard to believe that a team would axe their driver in such a way before the season had ended, and the fans were in shock and disbelief.

Lewis led the tributes afterwards. On Instagram he wrote, 'Daniel Ricciardo, it's been an honour to compete with you over the years, I'll never forget the battles, the laughs, and the drinking out of your shoe. It was gross, but I'm glad I got to do it with you bud.

'You leave a legacy of always being yourself, which in this sport is never easy. You've taken it all with the biggest smile, and I salute you for it. There is so much more for you up ahead, and I can't wait to see what you do next. Always here for you man.'

With many of the fans still angry with the strategy of starting with a soft tyre on Lewis's car, Mercedes were accused of favouring Russell, so in an effort to achieve harmony, Lewis released this statement: 'I know there has been a lot of chat about the last one, and our strategy in Singapore, which didn't work. When that happens it's natural to be frustrated, and easy for me to speak out in that frustration. We knew starting on the soft tyres was a bold and risky move, but one that could give us an advantage at the start, and I ultimately agreed with that recommendation. We also miscalculated what others might do.'

In that statement he was making it clear to disgruntled fans that, although things did not go according to plan, he was in complete harmony with the team, and he stressed that his support for the team, and theirs for him, would remain for the rest of the season. He wanted nothing more than that the fans would continue to support Mercedes, and by doing that, they were also supporting him.

During the period between the races, fans become easily bored, and journalists become even busier reporting on anything connected with F1. Guenther Steiner, ex team boss who was sacked by Haas, had brought out his memoirs. It was reported that he did not mince his words in referring to Abu Dhabi in 2021 and the controversial ending of the race, claiming that if Charlie Whiting, the former race director, who sadly passed away in 2019, had still been in charge, Hamilton would have undoubtedly been an eight time world champion. He stated that no matter who you were a fan of, that race was amazing entertainment, but from the regulations point of view, 'It was a s**t show of biblical proportions.'

Whilst many Formula One fans agreed with his remark, one wonders if it would have been much more beneficial, if Mr Steiner, and the many others who had since called Lewis the true eight time world champion, had stood up in support of him at the time instead of just accepting the result.

Mr Steiner followed up this remark with a humorous one, remarking about Hamilton's impending move to Ferrari. 'This guy will end up in the Vatican if he manages to bring success to Ferrari.'

On a beyond the grid podcast, he stated: 'I think he wants to try to do the magic, to bring Ferrari back to winning championships, and that is, I think, is his drive.'

Nigel Mansell has also shown his support of Lewis going to Ferrari, stating that he has always been a fan of Hamilton. He believes if Ferrari can give him a good car, then 'Lewis will be challenging for the championship in 2025.'

In the meantime, Lewis Hamilton has spoken out about his

own mental health issues, including depression. He admitted that he was as young as 13 when he first suffered from depression, with the pressures of racing, bullying at school, and feeling he had no one to talk to. As close as he is to his family, and the driving force that his father Anthony had been, he believed, like many men do, that showing his vulnerability was a sign of weakness.

He tried therapy, but didn't feel the experience was helpful, and he also tried silent retreats, and reading books about mental health. The pandemic was a difficult time for him and many others, so he tried going for a morning run to get in touch with his feelings.

A leading mental health charity has praised Sir Lewis for sharing his story. His intention was to let others who feel this way know that they are not alone. The charity believes many more men may seek help when they realise that even the most successful people in life can still have doubts in themselves, and struggle with feelings of depression.

25

Austin

A few hours before practice in Austin, FIA broke the news that one unnamed car was running a special ride height device or 'Bib'. Speculation was rife about this, and then Red Bull announced that it was them, but said they were not using it in parc fermé. The fans were really angry about this, as it was stated that Red Bull and the FIA were discussing it, whereas normally a team would be disqualified for such a move.

Zak Brown of McLaren was particularly vocal about it, stating he wanted to have further details about it, and both his drivers, Piastri and Norris, were not happy, as it might hinder their chances in competing for the title against Verstappen.

Ted Kravitz gave his take on it by saying he wondered why Verstappen didn't win his championships in the normal way.

When he was asked for his opinion, this is what Lewis said. 'I have only just heard about it before I got here. But I think the name of our sport is all about innovation. Red Bull have been the leaders, and they have innovated. Ultimately all the teams look at the rules, and try to find out how to massage those rules and get the most out of them. At the end of the day, they did a better job. God knows how long they have had that, and they've been winning championships. Maybe that stops now. . . I don't think that's the one thing that is going to stop them.'

During the only practice session they had before Sprint Qualifying, Lewis spun his car, but luckily was able to stay on track. Russell did the same, but also managed to keep it on track. By the end of the session, Sainz topped the time sheets with Leclerc 2nd, and Verstappen 3rd. Next came the McLaren's with Lewis in 6th and Russell in 7th. Once again the times had very small margins.

By the time qualifying came round, Lewis looked to be in a comfortable position to claim pole position by about 4 tenths of a second. But on his push lap there was a yellow flag, which totally ruined it for him, and he ended up 7th. Russell was 2nd with Verstappen on pole. Norris split the Ferraris in 4th, as they were 3rd and 5th.

Mercedes did not fare well in the race either. Lewis made up one place to 6th, and Russell was overtaken by the Ferraris and Norris, thus slipping down to 5th. It was clear the pace just was not there, so changes would need to be made to the set-ups before qualifying for the main race later in the day. Verstappen won the sprint race.

Later came qualifying for the main race on Sunday. Lewis had been particularly excited about racing in Texas, as he had a huge following there. So it was hugely disappointing for him to not make it out of Q1, and end up 18th. Later it was discovered that his car suspension was broken. Russell beached his car after claiming 6th position. Norris got pole.

Russell's crash had broken many of his new parts, so Lewis offered to let him have his updates, and even suggested to the

Lewis Fan Photographs

From top left: Rhian Adams, Josephine Jackson and son, Clare Boswell, Debbie White, Betty Waerzeggers' shoe signing by Lewis Hamilton.

team that if they changed the set-up of his car, which was not safe around bends, he would start from the pit lane and see if he could work his way up. But the team did not change his updates, and he lined up in 17th due to grid changes. Because the team had to work on Russell's car all night, he then had to start from the pit lane.

When the race started, Leclerc had an amazing start, moving him from 3rd into the lead. Lewis had a great start, and immediately made up 5 places to 12th, which was looking good. But on the 2nd lap, disaster struck, his car was on the gravel, and he was out of the race. Everyone was so shocked, and there was complete silence. Later, when interviewed, Toto admitted it was one hundred per cent the car; Lewis knows how to drive, but the new package was making it unstable around corners, and dangerous to drive. Russell had also crashed in qualifying, but was now running the older parts that had not been updated.

The Ferraris had a fine race. Leclerc was 1st, Sainz 2nd, Norris overtook Verstappen for 3rd, but the FIA then decided to give him a five second penalty for 'Pushing Verstappen off'. What was strange about that was, that at the beginning of the race, Verstappen had pushed Sainz off but was not penalised, and then later Russell pushed Bottas off, but was penalised with a five second penalty. One has to wonder why the stewards are not consistent with their decisions.

Russell managed to get himself up to 6th, but of course the fans were saying that Mercedes knew the update wasn't working, and this was why they did not take up Lewis's offer to swap. It was such a shame they did not trust the team that together with Lewis has enjoyed so much glory. It was only by letting Lewis run the new parts for the race that they could know for sure if they worked or not, and Toto was just as gutted as Lewis that he did not finish.

Toto spoke encouragingly to Lewis about the next race in Mexico. With just five races to go, Mercedes wanted Lewis to have more wins. Leaving Mercedes on a high note was the aim, so everyone hoped the fans would have something to be happy about during the coming weekend.

26

Mexico

During the week leading up to the Mexican Grand Prix, social media was alight with controversy regarding the move between Verstappen and Norris, where Verstappen had pushed him off the track, but it was Norris who had been penalised. Zak Brown was so angry about it, he decided to lodge an appeal to the FIA, but it was rejected, which is generally what happens after such an event.

Jensen Button had his say, stating that there should be a rule prohibiting drivers from pushing others off the track, as it appeared to be a grey area which Verstappen exploited whenever he was being challenged.

Lewis, as always, was asked his opinion, and the answer he gave was very frank. He found it very interesting that people are now talking about Verstappen's defending, because the same thing happened to him in 2021 many times during the season, and Verstappen was never punished. 'It's always been a grey area, this is why he got away with it for so long. They probably need to make adjustments for sure.'

The Briton also commented about the frequent change of stewards resulting in inconsistent decisions, stating that full time referees would be much better.

Later it was announced that the FIA would come up with revised wording to cover the specifics of the incident, and present it to the drivers for approval later this season.

Kimi Antonelli was due to run in practice 1 as is commonplace during the season, so Lewis wished him well, and sat out. Russell topped that session, and Kimi had a difficult drive, because he picked up some debris from the track.

Practice 2 didn't go too well, as Russell hit the kerb, and crashed out. Lewis finished in 7th place. Practice 3 was better for Lewis, he ended up 5th, some five tenths away from Piastri, who topped the session. Norris was 2nd, Sainz 3rd, Verstappen 4th. Russell was 8th.

In qualifying, Sainz got pole, Verstappen was 2nd, Norris 3rd, Leclerc 4th, Russell 5th and Lewis 6th. When interviewed afterwards, Lewis appeared a little glum, saying that he hoped he could make up some places on Sunday, as his qualifying just wasn't good, and he really didn't understand why.

Much had been made about Russell out-qualifying him this year, although on race day it was more often than not Lewis who has the strongest race pace and tyre management.

When the race started, Lewis overtook Russell for 5th, and up front Verstappen took Sainz for 1st place, doing his now signature move of running him off the track. There had been a lot of talk about this bending of the rules during the week, so later in the race, when Verstappen did it to Norris, the stewards reacted, and by the time he went for his pit stop, they had sanctioned Verstappen on two counts of ten second penalties for running other drivers off the track, and leaving it himself to gain an advantage. Later he was also given two points on his super licence.

After a while, Russell used DRS, and he passed Lewis again for 4th. Leclerc, who was running 2nd at the time, made an error and came off track, allowing Norris to then take 2nd place. Lewis and Russell duelled for position over many laps, but it was fair and clean racing, and in the end Russell had to concede 4th place to Lewis. They were both nursing damaged cars. Russell had damaged a wing when he hit a kerb, and Lewis had a hole in his floor which hindered his progress. So at the end of the race, they were both relieved to get their cars home and earn solid points.

Norris had complained about how dangerous Verstappen was. Now that other cars were as fast as his, he resorted to the same dirty tactics that he employed against Lewis during the infamous season of 2021. Finally, three years later, after overwhelming pressure from the drivers, team principals, and numerous disgruntled fans, they are addressing the problem. Some fans feel if they had acted in 2021 it would be a thing of the past, instead of a huge talking point. Verstappen did not accept any blame for his actions, because Horner never blamed him, but finally the FIA had punished him. We would see if that made any difference at the next race in Brazil.

27

Brazil

Brazil is a very important country for Sir Lewis Hamilton. It's the place he won his first world championship in 2008, his icon Ayrton Senna was Brazilian, and when he equalled Ayrton's pole positions he was presented with a special helmet. The Brazilian people have really taken him into their hearts, as in 2022 he was declared an honorary citizen.

It was announced on Wednesday 30th October, that to honour the 30th anniversary of Senna's death, Sir Lewis had been chosen to drive his McLaren car, and it would take place after the qualifying session on Saturday. This delighted his fans very much. It was a special honour, and when Lewis was told, he stated that he never believed in a million years that he would have the opportunity. But, in fact, he was the obvious choice, and no doubt the family of Senna probably had a lot to do with choosing him.

During the week, Mercedes announced that as they were not any longer fighting for a championship in 2024, they would use the remaining races for testing set-ups for their car to try and understand the dip in performance since the summer, and to get themselves back into competing for 2025.

This did not please the fans, as being the senior and more experienced driver, Lewis would be doing the testing. Many argued that surely Russell should do it, as Lewis wouldn't be there in 2025, but Lewis himself stated that he wanted the team he had such close ties with to perform well when he left it at the end of the season.

The weather forecast was for rain most of that weekend in Brazil, and in the past our valiant Briton had loved that, as the challenges it brings are exciting, and over the years he has won so many rain soaked races, it has earned him the name of 'rain master'. Silverstone in 2008 springs to mind, when in treacherous rain conditions he won the race by a margin of some 60 seconds.

But unfortunately that was not to be the case in Brazil. The team having opted for testing set-ups, gave him a car that was, in his own words, 'Undrivable!' Russell had a normal set-up, but Lewis described his car as like a plank of wood, stiff, unyielding on corners, and very dangerous. He had to work hard just to keep it out of the wall, so had no chance to drive fast.

In the sprint race, he qualified in 11th, and ended up in that position at the end of the race. Norris won the sprint after Piastri moved over to allow him to pass, so he could earn more championship points against Verstappen. Verstappen was 3rd, but later demoted to 4th after a safety car infringement.

Between the sessions came the special event when Sir Lewis would drive Senna's car of 1990. The crowd were in raptures as he drove around, and nobody even cared that it was pouring with rain. This winning car had been beautifully preserved for all these years, and it drove like a dream as he went around the track. The crowds paid homage and then cheered, waving their flags. Rain was not going to dampen their spirits! Then the Brazilian flag was given to Lewis and he held it out so the crowd could see as he drove round again. It was a history making moment, and a very poignant one, especially for the family of Senna. Senna's sister Viviane was there to give Lewis a hug of approval on such a landmark day. Lewis said afterwards that it had been an emotional moment for him, and he had actually done a couple more laps than they had meant him to.

After this came qualifying for the main race. Lewis suffered again, and he even berated his engineer for giving him such a dangerous car. It had never been known for him to complain so strongly before, but the weather was so bad, and he said he had absolutely no grip. After qualifying in 18th place, he said maybe he might start from the pit lane, which sounded a much better idea, because he would be able to take any new parts needed, and also maybe the team could change his set-up to a safe one.

Unfortunately, for whatever reason, he was not given that option, and after other penalties were applied from other drivers, he started the race from 14th, then spent all his time trying to keep the car from going into the wall, and it was amazing that he actually managed to finish in 10th place and grab himself a point.

Verstappen had a bad qualifying, starting from 17th, but with huge improvements made to his car, he was able to race up the grid to 1st place. This was similar to what Lewis did in 2021, after being sent to the back of the grid after the FIA decided to disqualify him because the height of a screw was deemed illegal. There had been a huge uproar at the time about this, but Lewis took his punishment on the chin and then raced to victory. Unfortunately, the car he was now driving was incapable of that, and it was very obvious that Mercedes would miss him a lot in 2025, as his skill and experience would be with another team.

The sad part about all this was that the man who had never given up in hard times had shown just how vulnerable he was right at this time. This was his statement after the races:

'The car I have right now is the worst I have ever driven. I don't care whether I finish ahead of George or not in the championship. I just want to keep the car out of the wall, and try to score points for the team. If I can finish well and they give me a car that doesn't bounce off the track in the next few races, then hopefully we will get a better result. Whatever, but yeah, looking forward to Christmas.'

Fans remained very loyal to him, and they felt his honesty in telling his team early that he was leaving at the end of the year had not helped him. But with three races to go, they hoped he would bounce back, and be given a car that was safe to drive so he could end his time with Mercedes on a much more positive note.

28

Controversy Continues

It was inevitable, after his race in Brazil, that Sir Lewis would be verbally attacked and accused of 'Being past his shelf life.' Surprisingly, those words came from Toto Wolff, who explained that, like a football manager, he had to be aware of new talent, and with Lewis going to Ferrari it would solve his problem of having to tell an icon that his time was up.

His words have angered many fans, and were so unexpected because their relationship was close. But people believed Toto was trying to save face because they still could not get the car right, and it's no wonder that Lewis was finally leaving.

Bernie Eccleston has jumped on the band wagon, saying: 'Hamilton should tear up his Ferrari contract and retire.' Then Jeremy Clarkson also said he was now past it, and should retire. They had quickly forgotten his epic win at Silverstone, followed by Belgium, at a time when the car was actually running competitively. But the fans don't forget, and Fred Vasseur of Ferrari said he cannot wait to have Lewis in his team next year.

Sir Lewis wrote the foreword for a new Schumacher book, and it is interesting that George Russell made these comments:

'Lewis did a great job. But from one legend to another, I have proven to be on Lewis's level with my two race wins, so in a sense I'm on Schumacher's level. I would have been honoured to do the foreword as well.'

These remarks caused a lot of hilarity amongst the fans, as Russell has two wins, against 105, and has yet to win a world championship. It is always great for young drivers to have a confidence in themselves, and maybe in the future he might be a threat, but many fans wondered if he was actually joking.

All these remarks are actually good for Lewis, as he has always stated that he feeds on negativity, and he loves to prove people wrong. Recently reactions of drivers at the start of a race were tested, and Lewis was faster than anyone. So age is just a number for him, and turning 40 next year will not quench the fire inside him to win races.

As I stated previously, Lewis Hamilton fans are a force of nature themselves. He is hated by some people, but they are the minority. His fans are passionate, and do not take kindly to anyone who they feel is disrespecting him. Lewis himself knows that if he is not winning races, he will always be scrutinised, but he is always self critical, and will strive to do better. When he had a good result, he had always been quick to praise his team of engineers. Indeed, he respected them all so much that he planned to do a farewell tour of all the factories to thank them for the support they gave him over the past twelve years.

Gunther Steiner had shown himself to be a man with a great sense of humour. When he was told that Lewis Hamilton would now be left out of meetings in case he took valuable data information to Ferrari, this was what he said:

'The car is not the best. It's about the 4th best car, and Lewis can complain because he is leaving. George has to show he is a team leader in the future, because when his contract is up, his seat is not one hundred per cent safe.'

When asked if Mercedes should be worried about the 'valuable IP', he laughed. 'Nobody wants it! Maybe they want to know what not to do. Toto said the car was sorted back in the summer, but it wasn't.'

But in spite of all this, Lewis Hamilton explained that he was still in love with his team, and that would never change, it was just that he wanted a new challenge. In the past, Toto had told him he was a lot more than a racing driver, and James Allison also explained how Lewis always paid attention to every little detail with precision when experimenting with the car, which he had never seen any other driver do. So with three more races to go, the time was fast approaching for the final lap with Mercedes. Lewis and his fans would want it to be a lap to remember.

In the meantime, after a huge backlash from the fans after his remarks, Toto Wolff insisted his words had been taken out of context. He emphasised that Hamilton remained one of the sport's best; especially when he was given the right machinery.

'Contrary to my own self-assessment, we see with Lewis that he is very much there when the car is right, and we have not been able to give him the car to perform his best. And that is a frustration that we equally have in the team and for him.'

He then added, "He's very sharp. He's different to when he was a 20 year old, but his experience and his race craft are tremendous.'

Whether these remarks would be enough to calm the fans remained to be seen.

29

Las Vegas

Lewis was interviewed soon after arriving at Las Vegas, and asked if he felt he had to prove anything to Toto this weekend. His response was calm and measured; he seemed completely unruffled by the question, explaining he was feeling very fit, and had trained hard. He also explained that due to his longevity, he knew that many different things had been written about him, but was committed to giving his all for the last three races with Mercedes. This was in response to the people who had accused him of 'checking out'.

Practice 1 and 2 were held in much cooler conditions than usual, but it seemed to suit his car. He topped the first session by 4 tenths of a second to his team mate Russell, who could not match him, even after having a tow. He then topped the second session by a finer margin to Norris, with Russell 3rd, some two tenths behind him. When interviewed, he explained that this was the first time this year his car had been easy to drive in both sessions. But he was cautious, saying that the race pace was not as strong as the single lap pace, and adjustments would need to be made before qualifying to improve it.

Later, in qualifying, both Mercedes' drivers found

themselves leading the time sheets. By the time Q3 came round, everything changed. Russell took pole, Lewis had topped Q2, but, once again, everything changed in Q3 for him. Lewis had to abort his first lap after a front left lock-up. On his second attempt, he lost the back end and had to settle for 10th position. It was described as a rare mistake from Hamilton, but when interviewed, a downcast Lewis insisted that the handling of his car changed in Q3, making it much harder for him to keep it on track. He said he would do his utmost to get higher up the grid in the race.

Toto Wolff admitted that Mercedes had no idea why their car was suddenly so fast, suggesting it might have something to do with the cooler evening conditions. Lewis was angry with himself for not qualifying higher, whereas Russell was confident he could win the race when starting on pole.

Lewis made a cautious start, and was up to 8th position by lap 9. Then came the first round of pit stops, and his overtaking, so by lap 11 he was in 3rd position. When he made his pit stop, he came out in 9th, and had work to do all over again. But there was no stopping our Briton. With a newly found confidence in his car, he gradually picked off all his rivals, and was setting qualifying laps through most of the race to end up in 2nd position. That was his emphatic answer to anyone who believed he was 'past his sell by date'.

Russell took his 2nd win of 2024, and although Leclerc had been in 2nd position at one point, tyre wear slowed him down, so Sainz completed the podium, Leclerc had to settle for 4th. Verstappen was 5th, but it gave him enough points to become champion for the 4th year running. Sir Lewis was one of the first to congratulate him and his team. What was a nice gesture, was the engineers in Red Bull patting Lewis Hamilton on the back, and congratulating him on his masterful drive from 10th to 2nd place on a track where it was very difficult to overtake safely. Lewis also praised Russell for his win.

The fans were delighted with his drive from 10th place to 2nd place, so they voted Lewis Hamilton the Driver of the Day.

Mercedes were scratching their heads as to why their car was not performing well during the previous week, and at the same time were still scratching their heads to know exactly why it had suddenly become so fast. The fans just hoped it remained that way for the last two races, but with Formula One anything can happen.

30

The Hamilton Commission

Mercedes arranged a competition for fans to enter, and 150 of them would have their names on the car when Lewis did his last race for the team at Abu Dhabi. Lewis himself thought this a great idea, remarking how Team LH had always been there to support him, and how nice it would be to have names up there on the car. This created great excitement amongst his fan base, with many hoping they would be one of the lucky ones.

The last two races were just one week apart, with the final being in Abu Dhabi on 8th December. With Verstappen already claiming his 4th successive title, there was no pressure, but it was now a contest between Ferrari and McLaren for 1st place in the Constructors' Championship, as there were only a few points between them, and position is everything. Toto Wolff was hoping for a good showing in Qatar, having enjoyed the unexpected surprise of having both of his drivers take 1st and 2nd in Las Vegas.

Instead of doing testing in Abu Dhabi after the final race had taken place, Lewis had decided he wanted to do a farewell tour to all the factories concerned, to thank them for their support over the last twelve years. There were many disappointed fans, who wanted to see him testing in a Ferrari, but he wanted to end his association with Mercedes in what he felt was the right way.

Indeed, Ferrari had released Carlos Sainz so that he could go and test in a Williams, which would be his new team in 2025, but when questioned during the press conference at Las Vegas, Fred insisted that he fully understood Lewis still had commitments that he wanted to honour, and he also explained that he was happy to release Carlos after the last race so that he could do testing. It was believed that Lewis would get the opportunity to test a Ferrari sometime in January.

This was a social media announcement from Sir Lewis Hamilton:

'I launched the Hamilton Commission in 2021to figure out why there were so few people who looked like me in the sport, and why it's been that way for all of my life. With the help of the Royal Academy of Engineering, we started answering those questions and created a report outlining what the barriers were for people like me. This charter is a result of those findings from that report. The impact this can have is massive, and I thank the sport for taking on this commitment. For all the teams, Formula One, and the FIA to recognise the need for diversity is an incredible sign of progress. Can't wait to see and support all that comes from this.'

His words were in response to even more progress with Mission 44, his charity, which was created in 2021. Formula One, the FIA, and all ten of the teams agreed to a new charter. This is a result of recommendations from a report that seeks the motor sport sector to improve diversity and inclusion with collaboration, so that motor sport will embrace diversity.

The Formula One community was recognising how important diversity is, allowing new ideas, innovation, and culture to enrich the sport. Sir Lewis Hamilton had worked hard to make all this happen, because, when he entered the sport, it was difficult for him being the only black driver, and he wants anyone from an ethnic background to feel as included as anyone else, and to have the same opportunities to succeed, either on the track, or working behind the scenes in the garages or factories.

Now that he had the backing of Formula One, it spoke volumes about his sincerity to make changes and their willingness to be involved. Once again he faced criticism from those who felt he should do nothing more than just drive his car, but that would not hold him back from doing what he felt was right.

It was good news to note that, during recent years, all the teams and stakeholders in Formula One had acted to provide ways of improving diversity and access, and provided opportunities within the sport. Stefan Domencali, President and CEO of Formula One, had said:

'Our sport is rightly recognised for its elite performance and innovation, and we are clear that the only way to maintain and improve those exceptional standards is to welcome diversity of thought, ideas, and experiences. The sport is fiercely competitive, and we're all committed to employing the very best talent. We know from the Hamilton Commission Report that there are opportunities for us to work collectively to both find, and nurture that talent, and across the sport, significant change has already taken place. The charter is the next important milestone on that journey, and we are all committed to making our sport more open and diverse.'

Mohammed Ben Sulayem. President of the FIA, also responded:

f

'The diversification of motor sport is paramount to its continued success. Through ensuring equal opportunity for equal talent, increasing accessibility, and joining together in our commitment to uphold this charter, we will drive forward change. This landmark partnership between Formula One, the teams, and our Federation, signifies a united course of action, which I am proud to be a part of.'

Dr Hayaatun Sillum CBE, Chief Executive of the Royal Academy of Engineering said:

'Formula One took the findings of the Hamilton Commission in 2021 very seriously, and since then the sport has created a range of initiatives to increase diversity. This charter, which the sport commissioned us to create independently, sets a framework for progress and establishes commitment to both principles, and action. It is a key step in F1's ongoing efforts to improve access and performance, and we believe it will be a catalyst for even more positive impact and cross sport working.'

Another change that Lewis Hamilton had been speaking out about was that there should be a Formula One race in Africa. He had been vociferous about this for some time, and Stefan Domenicali confirmed that the FIA had been listening to him. He hoped that the first race there could take place before Lewis Hamilton retires.

When Sir Lewis Hamilton decides it's time to retire, all these innovations he has achieved will definitely leave a lasting legacy of his time in the sport. Whether fans approve or not, he has helped to bring Formula One into the 21st century, because there has been a need for change, and he has been instrumental in achieving it.

31

Qatar

After the success at Las Vegas, Mercedes said they were determined to put up a good showing in Qatar. Lewis once again affirmed his commitment to the team, and both drivers said how much they were looking forward to getting back out on the track.

During practice, neither of the cars looked particularly fast, and as it was a sprint weekend, it did not allow much time to set them up, because qualifying was to take place within a few hours. Both cars made it into Q3, but then, frustratingly, as has happened so many times this year, Lewis found himself down in 7th place, and Russell made it into 2nd. When interviewed after, a downcast Lewis admitted he had no idea why the car behaved this way in Q3, and he was slow. It was clear after three years of struggles with an unco-operative car, he has had enough.

During this week the car was lacking pace. Lewis did manage a great start, gaining two places past Verstappen and Leclerc, but after a while Leclerc overtook him, and when the race ended, Lewis was one position higher in 6th. Russell slipped down a place, finishing in 3rd. The sprint was won by

Piastri with Norris 2nd, Verstappen had a bad race ending in 8th position.

During qualifying for the main race, Verstappen recovered from his bad sprint race to get pole, Russell was 2nd, and Lewis came 6th. In spite of his disappointment, Lewis vowed to give his all. Later Verstappen was slapped with a one place penalty for driving too slowly, and Russell was promoted to pole position.

But this race was to be a disaster for Mercedes. Lewis did an accidental false start, which relegated him down to 9th position, and then he got a five second penalty. Later in the race he got a puncture from debris on the track, and had to do another pit stop, then just after that there was a safety car, so he lost the opportunity to get a free pit stop. To add to that he was noted for speeding in the pit lane and was handed a drive through penalty, which ended any hopes he had of making progress. At one point he wanted to retire the car, but Bono said no, so he served his penalty, then was told he could retire the car, but Lewis battled on, finishing in 12th place. He apologised to his team for the false start, and the pit lane infringement. Russell was overtaken by Verstappen and Norris at the start, relegating him to 3rd place. He had no pace in his car, and slipped down to 7th place at one point. Later, because of retirements, he was 5th and then Norris was given a ten second penalty, which elevated Russell to 4th place.

However, both drivers had once again found the car very hard to drive. This was not the result that anyone wanted. When races go wrong, tension is high at the time, and one can only imagine how disappointed the whole team, who all contributed to win races, must feel. Naturally the fans feel disappointed and let down when their driver is given no chance to do well, especially in the case of Lewis, who had such little time left at Mercedes.

When emotions had calmed down, and the drivers could reflect on their race, common sense prevailed. After the race, this is what Lewis had to say:

'This weekend has not been great, but we have another week next week where we can try to finish a bit better, and I hope we do have a better result. These last races don't have an impact on all the great things we have done together as a team. Races are a roller coaster ride of emotions. I've had great races in my life, and bad races too. Ultimately it's not how you fall, it's how you get back up, and we will try again next week.'

Andrew Shovlin added. 'There's plenty for us to learn in order to improve, and we will be focused on doing so as we prepare for the final race of the season in Abu Dhabi, and what we hope will be a fitting farewell for Lewis.'

Lewis would be hoping that his fans would unite behind him and Mercedes for the last race, because no matter how rocky the road had been for him during those last three years, he would always consider Mercedes his family, and like all families, they can fall out with one another, but the love remains forever.

33

Abu Dhabi

THE FINAL LAP

Social media was full of posts about Lewis Hamilton leaving Mercedes during the week leading up to the last race. Nostalgic posts stating it was the end of a very special era. Here is one of them.

'Sir Lewis Hamilton this week will race his last race with the Mercedes squadron after 12 seasons, 245 Grand Prizes, 84 victories, 79 pole positions, 153 podiums, 6 championships and priceless moments full of happiness and excitement. The most successful combination between a driver and a team in the entire history of Formula 1: LAST EPISODE OF A LEGENDARY STORY!'

In his preview of the Abu Dhabi Grand Prix, Toto Wolff had this to say about the very special partnership that comes to an end on Sunday:

'After twelve incredible years we get ready to write the final chapter in our racing story with Lewis this weekend. It has been quite a journey. When we first started working together in 2013, we couldn't have imagined what was to come.

'Six drivers' world championships, eight constructor's titles, and much more. The most successful driver and team partnership in F1 history. Many highs that we have enjoyed, some crushing lows that we've overcome together.

'Our relationship has meant so much more than numbers and statistics though. It is a legacy that transcends our sport, with a lasting impact beyond the race track. One that has strived to increase diversity in our sport. To fight for inclusion. Lewis has been the catalyst for so much of this, and we have been honoured, and proud, to work hand in hand with him. That work won't stop at the end of the year. But it began because of the impetus led by Lewis.

'This weekend is a celebration. A celebration of everything we have accomplished together. Lewis's association with Mercedes goes back 26 years. Every lap of his career so far has been powered by the three pointed star.

'We will honour this unparalleled story in Abu Dhabi and across the following week as we visit Kuala Lumpur, Stuttgart, then finally Brixworth and Brackley. And honour it knowing that, while this phase of our relationship is coming to an end, Lewis will always be part of our family. For now though, our full focus is on the race weekend. There is no better way to mark the end of our time together than with a strong performance on the track. The entire team is focused on adding one more highlight to the reel. We will also want to end the season on the front foot.

'Thank you Lewis, for one final time, let's do this.'

George Russell had this to say: 'I have learned a lot from Lewis, and I feel very grateful to have been his team mate. He is one of the greatest drivers of all time, and being able to work with him, and having him as a reference has been extremely valuable for my career.'

Mercedes Petronas compiled a special promotional video of some of Sir Lewis Hamilton's most iconic moments, narrated by young boys, who have been inspired by him. It quickly dominated social media, viewed by millions of people.

Sir Lewis had his photograph taken with his team of engineers, and then released his own emotional statement:

'This is really it. My last race with Mercedes. What we've built together over the years is nothing short of historic. People doubted me making this move in 2013, and here we are now. The records we've broken, the championships we've won, it all speaks for itself. This won't be the last time I thank Mercedes, but going into my final race with the team is really hitting me now. It's really the end of an era in my life, in my career, for the team, and in F1 history. I'm proud of what we have created, I'm proud of every single person that has been a part of this with me. Thank you, it's been real, now let's go again one more time.'

On the 5th December news came that Mercedes had launched a global campaign to celebrate Lewis Hamilton's legacy with the team.

It would feature iconic photos of Lewis, which would light up landmarks in Kuala Lumpur, the UK, and USA, to include Times Square. During the Abu Dhabi weekend, Hamilton would carry the campaign message on his car, together with the names of 150 of his fans, honouring and representing his millions of loyal supporters.

Partner Whatsapp would feature a special message on his clothes, which culminated in a farewell to team mates at the end of the week. As quoted: 'We will honour the remarkable role Lewis has played in our team, and the defining achievements of his years with us.'

This had been created in collaboration with the London based agency AMV BBDO, and was entitled 'Every dream needs a team', paying tribute to his record breaking career. The aim being to connect the young driver's dreams of F1 glory, with the aspirations of the new generation inspired by him.

This campaign underscored a core truth of this sport which Lewis has always championed, and he included everyone when he said, "We win and lose together."

His team reflected: 'Lewis has achieved every dream possible with Mercedes. But as he moves to Maranello with our deepest gratitude, we begin a new chapter of our journey.' But Mercedes have made their message clear. 'Thank you, Lewis.'

James Vowles, who now leads the Williams team, worked with Lewis Hamilton for many years. This was his tribute to him:

"I'd start with this. I am the man I am today thanks to Lewis. He taught me about how you can re-invent yourself every single year. Continuous change, continuous improvement, continuous evolution. Don't accept what you knew six months ago, accept where you want to be in six months time.

'And he embodies that far more than any other individual I've ever met. He reinvented how he trains, how he looks at videos, how he looks at data, how he works with engineers, how he finds head space. And that's really hard to do. If you think about what that really means, you're winning multiple world championships, and yet you question everything at the end of the year. It led me into the same sort of mindset. I am the human being I am today thanks to him. We had some incredible times – personal and on the track, and I can only wish him all the best in his future with Ferrari, and I think he'll be brilliant.'

Right up until there was action on the track, tributes were pouring in, and emotions were high amongst Lewis Hamilton fans, for although he was not leaving yet, it reminded them that he would not be around forever. Right now, however, he was merely changing teams. The desire to see him go out on a high note in his final lap with Mercedes was imperative for the fans, and social media was alight with pleas from the fans to Mercedes to give Lewis a car to fight with this final time.

During practice it looked as if the pleas from the fans may have been answered, as Lewis looked very fast in all sessions, and beat his team mate in every session. Excitement amongst his followers was growing; could he end his iconic time at Mercedes in the best way possible?

But as has happened at other times this year, fate was not on the Briton's side. Hulkenberg hit a bollard during qualifying which lodged itself under Lewis's car, so with performance now gone, he had to settle for 18th position. The fans were mortified at such bad luck, although Lewis himself was composed when being interviewed afterwards. He explained it was disappointing, as his car seemed to have good pace.

Later Toto took full responsibility for sending him out at the wrong time, and after holding his head in his hands he was full of anguish. His apology to Lewis was heartfelt. He explained they had sent him out too late, and there was no time left to do another lap. He also commented they had given him the best car set-up, and as he was visibly quicker than Russell all weekend, fans were left wondering if he had been given slower set-ups all year until the last race, which would explain why he had trouble qualifying. Maybe it was important for Mercedes to give Russell the best set-up, as he would be their lead driver next year.

The fans were so frustrated, and their anger was directed towards Toto and the team, because all their hopes for Lewis had evaporated so quickly. But, of course, nobody could have known that the bollard would fly underneath his car. It was just another hurdle for Lewis to overcome, and he would once again have to fight his way up the grid to achieve any sort of decent result.

On race day the weather was fine. When Lewis was interviewed during the drivers' parade he was excited for the challenge of fighting from the back of the grid, and vowed to put on a good show in his last race.

He started from 16th position, and was up to 12th by lap three. By lap eighteen he was 6th. In the meantime there were incidents with Verstappen and Piastri, which resulted in Verstappen getting a ten second penalty. Piastri made a sarcastic remark about it being a champion's drive, but later he also had an incident, and earned his own ten second penalty.

What the fans wanted more than ever, was to hear Bono tell Lewis it was now hammer time, a phrase that had been used so much in the past, but not lately because the car just had not been fast enough. So when Bono came over the radio to tell him that his team mate was 14 seconds up the road, but because his pace was so strong, he could beat him, our fearless Briton set to work to hunt him down.

Lewis drove his heart out, whilst the fans watched with bated breath as the gap came down. Then, on the very last lap, Lewis made his move, he passed Russell, sweeping round the outside, and George on worn hard tyres simply had no answer for him. He had raced from 16th position to 4th, just missing out on the podium, but definitely out-driving the car. Norris was 1st, Sainz 2nd, and a fine drive from 19th gave Leclerc 3rd and Driver of the Day. But it was McLaren who won the Constructors' Championship, and Norris confirmed that he would be celebrating that with his team principal Zak Brown later.

Toto praised Lewis highly, calling it a drive of a champion, and Bono came on the radio, his voice clearly charged with emotion, saying. 'It's been a pleasure to work with you mate.' Lewis, sounding equally emotional, then thanked him and everyone from the Mercedes team for helping him to achieve all the success he has had.

Mark Webber hailed him not just as a driver, but also as a person who cares about others, and wants to make a better future which is inclusive for everyone.

Lewis himself was interviewed, and he seemed to be taken aback about all the love that had been showered on him. In spite of his epic success, he remains a very humble man, and seems unaware what sort of global impact he has made. There were crowds of excited fans following behind as Channel 4 representatives walked through the paddock talking to him, and the outpouring of love was clear for everyone to see.

Later, when the Channel 4 pundits were reflecting on the best moment of the year, consensus of opinion was Lewis's iconic win at Silverstone.

Fans will not see Lewis in a Ferrari until February 2025, as he is first touring all the Mercedes factories to say goodbye and thank everyone for their part in helping him achieve his dreams.

With Ferrari he will be dressed in red, and he says, whereas in the past he wanted to be remembered for his driving and race wins, he now hopes he will be remembered for his work in Mission 44, and inclusion. He does not want anyone to go through the bullying and racial prejudice that he did as a child.

All his fans will be wishing him well at Ferrari, and if they give him a good car, he will be fighting for his eighth championship. This was something Toto wanted him to win at Mercedes, and maybe he could have done if they had given him a longer contract, as rules change again 2026. But Ferrari have offered him a longer contract, and an ambassador role, so Mercedes' loss is Ferrari's gain. Mark Webber recently stated: 'Sir Lewis Hamilton is Formula One,' and few can argue with that. Stats don't lie.

Even David Coulthard has had to change his opinion of Lewis, as he stated after the race: 'Lewis is the most influential driver in the history of the sport in terms of what he has done, and anyone who denies his greatness is delusional.' Seeing as Coulthard is an ambassador for Red Bull, and a fan of Verstappen, this is a clear message to the haters, who try to diminish the achievements of Lewis in social media posts. The truth is that many of the cruel comments are delusional.

That last race with Mercedes saw the end of a very special era, onwards and upwards Sir Lewis, we win and lose together.

He completed his final lap with Mercedes, and now his journey goes on. He once said when somebody asked if he was retiring.

'I am working on a masterpiece, I will decide when it's done!'